GLOBAL SOCIAL GOVERNANCE

– Themes and Prospects

Bob Deacon, Eeva Ollila,
Meri Koivusalo and Paul Stubbs

Globalism and Social Policy Programme, 2003

ISBN 951-724-399-5

Cover photo: Vietnam/Riku Cajander

Hakapaino Oy
Helsinki 2003

Preface

In today's world of globalisation, individual national societies cannot be understood in isolation from the processes occurring at the supranational level. National public policies and practices are always influenced by global factors. It is, however, clear that the relative roles of the different global parties involved in managing globalisation are in flux. International organisations dealing with economic, trade and financial policies seem to have ever-increasing visibility and power compared with those that deal with the social dimensions of globalisation.

This issue also poses great challenges from the point of view of the Ministry for Foreign Affairs of Finland (MFAF). Finland's President Tarja Halonen currently co-chairs the work of the World Commission for the Social Dimensions of Globalisation, initiated by the ILO.

Economic and social aspects are nevertheless two inseparable "sides of the same coin" and there must be a sound balance between the two. At the same time as the process of industrialisation presented unforeseen opportunities for productivity and growth over the last couple of centuries, the socially unacceptable side-effects of industrialisation created tensions that had to be alleviated. The combination of the threat of political instability (revolution) and innovative social reformist thinking led to the emergence of institutional social policies at national and local levels. Today, with globalisation promising unforeseen gains in economic efficiency, there is an urgent need for innovative and effective institutional social policies at the global level. Unless a balance is found between the economic and the social dimensions, the promises of today's globalisation will not be realised.

In order to encourage and enrich discussion about the balanced and democratic governance of globalisation, the MFAF commissioned four studies from the Globalism and Social Policy Programme (GASPP), which is a collaborative research programme of Finland's STAKES[1] and the University of Sheffield. The topics of the four studies were: global social governance reform, public-private partnerships in the health area, the health implications of World Trade Organization (WTO) agreements, and the role of international non-governmental actors in social development policy.

Professor Bob Deacon's work on global governance reform concludes that it would be possible, and in line with the basic values of Finnish and like-minded governments' policies, to take an increasingly active role in improving global social governance. Finland and other countries with similar views should aim for globalisation to be more equitable and more socially regulated, and for the United Nations to have a more powerful role in global economic and social affairs in comparison with the international financial institutions. Yet, while reform of global institutions and policies is clearly needed, Deacon believes that ad hoc networks and partnerships can also be effective ways to build global political alliances. Deacon recommends that the empowerment of the South in international decision-making processes should remain on Finland's agenda. The introduction of new international taxation to pay for global public goods is also an issue that must be kept in focus.

---

[1] "STAKES" =The National Research and Development Centre for Welfare and Health

Dr. Eeva Ollila's work describes the increasing development towards interaction and partnerships between the corporate sector and the UN. She concludes that global public-private partnerships in health-related areas tend not to integrate well with other ongoing horizontal processes. Instead, they tend to build up vertical structures and lead to fragmented and technology-driven health policies, undermining both institutional development of health systems and the role of the relevant UN agencies. In line with the principle that funding for public-private partnerships should be additional to development funding, she recommends that development aid money should not be diverted from its traditional channels to public-private partnerships.

Dr. Meri Koivusalo analyses the role and relevance of trade agreements hosted by the World Trade Organisation from the point of view of health policy. Emphasising the aspects that are particularly important for developing countries, she looks at issues in which trade and health policies are in conflict. She is concerned that European positions are too biased towards the interests of Europe's export industries, while health, nutrition, consumption and development policy perspectives receive only limited attention. She argues for more coherence in European external policies.

Dr. Paul Stubbs rethinks the role of international non-governmental actors in social development work and in social policy development. He believes that these parties could do more than act as sub-contractors for government-funded projects. They should play a more progressive role, helping to get key local organisations, groups and individuals more involved in the process of making social policy. Dr. Stubbs also suggests a range of quality control measures for NGO work, and recommends a conceptual shift away from poverty reduction, towards the analysis and advocacy of livelihoods, social justice and social rights.

All these papers recommend the strengthening of Southern perspectives and roles in matters of global governance. Another common theme is the argument for coherence between policies that address the various dimensions of globalisation. This means that the positions taken by Finland and other like-minded governments, whether at the EU, UN, World Bank or the WTO, and whether about development, health, social security, finance or trade, should be informed by common thinking and common values seeking to promote more equitable, rule-based, globalisation.

The Ministry for Foreign Affairs of Finland wishes to thank the GASPP team for enriching Finnish and broader international debates on these important social governance issues. Finland is increasingly engaged in macro-policy discussions regarding the contents and priorities of the national poverty reduction strategies of our partner countries. These macro-policy dialogues are too often dominated by an unbalanced, sometimes ideological, economic policy perspective. In the interest of balance we welcome the further strengthening of 'social policy voices' in these processes. It is necessary to note that the perspectives outlined on this publications are entirely those of the GASPP researchers, and do not necessarily represent the views of the MFAF. In any case, however, they provide valuable "elements for discussion", which is exactly the purpose of this series of publications.

Timo Voipio
Social Development Adviser
Ministry for Foreign Affairs of Finland

Contents

Acronyms

ASEAN	Association of South East Asian Nations
BiH	Bosnia-Herzegovina
CIPR	Commission on Intellectual Property Rights (UK)
CMH	Commission on Macroeconomics and Health
EB	Executive Board
EC	European Commission
EBRD	European Bank for Reconstruction and Development
ECOSOC	Economic and Social Council of the United Nations
EPHA	European Public Health Alliance
EU	European Union
FCTC	Framework Convention on Tobacco Control
FTAA	Free Trade Area of the Americas
GA	General Assembly
GAIN	Global Alliance for Improved Nutrition
GATS	General Agreement on Trade in Services
GATT	General Agreement on Tariffs and Trade
GAVI	Global Alliance for Vaccine Initiative
GFATM	Global Fund to Fight AIDS, Tuberculosis and Malaria
GHPPP	Global health-related public-private partnerships
ICC	international consulting company
ICFTU	International Confederation of Free Trade Unions
ICPD	International Conference on Population and Development
ICSID	International Centre for Settlement of Investment Disputes
ICSW	International Council on Social Welfare
ILO	International Labour Organisation
IMF	International Monetary Fund
INGO	international non-governmental organization
ISPO	International Simeltaneous Policy Organisation
JIU	Joint Inspection Unit (of the United Nations)
MERCOSUR	Common Market of the South (*Spanish acronym*)
NGO	non-governmental organization
OECD	Organization for Economic Cooperation and Development
ODA	official development assistance
PPP	public-private partnerships
PRSP	Poverty Reduction Strategy Paper
SADC	South African Development Community

SPS	Sanitary and Phytosanitary Measures (Agreement)
TABD	Transatlantic Business Dialogue
TACD	Trans Atlantic Consumer Dialogue
TNC	transnational corporation
TNI	Transnational Institute
TRIPS	Trade-Related Aspects of Intellectual Property Rights
TWN	Third World Network
UNAIDS	Joint United Nations Programme on HIV/AIDS
UNCTAD	United Nations Conference on Trade and Development
UNDESA	United Nations Department of Economic and Social Affairs
UNFIP	The United Nations Fund for International Partnerships
UNFPA	United Nations Population Fund
UNICEF	United Nations Children's Fund
UNRISD	United Nations Research Institute for Social Development
USAID	The United States Agency for International Development
WHA	World Health Assembly
WHO	World Health Organization
WIPO	World Intellectual Property Organisation
WTO	World Trade Organization

I
GLOBAL SOCIAL GOVERNANCE REFORM:
From Institutions and Policies to Networks, Projects and Partnerships

Bob Deacon

Professor of International Social Policy
Director of Globalism and Social Policy Programme (GASPP)
University of Sheffield and STAKES

1. Summary and overview

This chapter addresses the prospects for improved social governance at the global level. It begins with an examination of the concept of globalisation and how globalisation has both affected the making of national social policy and introduced an era of global social policy making even though the institutional capacity to make global social policy is far from adequate. It then turns to some of the Global Social Governance reform issues that have arisen in this new era. It continues with a review of the Global Governance Reform Players, and notes the Forums where debate about these issues take place. It then sets out some ambitious approaches to Global Institutional Reform and assesses the institutional and political obstacles to such a major reform. The chapter continues by describing a modest set of feasible Global Social Governance Reforms.

It concludes, however, by focusing not on the reform of institutions or policies but on new international policy action and implementation processes that seem to be enabling international stakeholders to by-pass ossified institutional structures and the current impasse in policy debates. This is followed by suggestions and recommendations as to how Finland and other like-minded developed Northern countries might best advance global social governance reform in the direction of a rules-based and equitable world order in the light of this analysis.

The message of the chapter is that, while there are on the international policy agenda a number of worthy and desirable *institutional* reforms that should be implemented at the global level and while the struggle to shift global *policy* from its neo-liberal character to something more socially responsible continues, the actual focus of much international effort to improve the world's management of global social issues is centred upon *networks*, *partnerships* and *projects*. The question for

Finland and like-minded countries is how it positions itself in relation to these activities. The brief concludes with three principles that might enable Finland and like-minded countries to have the influence they would wish both at the traditional levels of *institutional reform* and *policy change* and enable them to engage with emerging *networks, partnerships and projects.* If policy-making has shifted to this new *network* arena, then *global political alliances* need to be fashioned to enable these networks also to be guided by principles rather than pragmatism. These principles entail:

1. Forging alliances with global Southern country partners and groups within which Southern voices are heard.
2. Supporting approaches to world regionalism within which the social dimension of trading arrangements is given due attention.
3. Working always to achieve a more equitable access to services and provision.
4. Establishing within-country policy synergy towards global questions across all Ministries.

2. Globalisation, global social policy, global governance

2.1 Globalisation

There is no globally accepted definition of globalisation and, in practice, the term has been applied to a wide range of unrelated phenomena.

> Due to irreconcilable definitions many globalisation debates are stalemated from the outset... (globalisation has been defined as)... internationalism, liberalisation, universalisation, modernisation/ westernisation, deterritorialisation.
>
> (Scholte 2000)

What consensus there is among social scientists suggests that globalisation means a shrinking of time and space; an ever closer connection between economic and social actors and events in different parts of the world.

> Globalisation may be thought of initially as a widening, deepening and speeding up of world-wide interconnectedness in all aspects of contemporary life.
>
> (Held and McGrew 1999)

> (Globalisation involves)... tendencies to a world-wide reach, impact, or connectedness of social phenomena or to a world-encompassing awareness among social actors...
>
> (Therborn 2000)

Informational and communation technologies are usually placed at the heart of this process of time and space shrinkage (Castells, 1996). There is also wide agreement that there are various dimensions to globalisation: economic, political, social, cultural and environmental.

Although there is nothing in the above definitions to suggest that globalisation is inherently bad or harmful, its effects are hotly disputed, particularly with regard to their impact on welfare systems (Mishra 1999). Perspectives on the benefits or otherwise of globalisation range from the 'hyperglobalisers' celebrating the domination and power for good of the globalised economy and free markets and their associated institutions of global financial governance; to the 'sceptics', who argue that the case is overstated and that the world is only globally interconnected in financial terms; and to the 'transformationalists', who see globalisation as a long-term historical process with which governments and people are faced, the nature of which is contested (Held et al 1999).

The related dispute within political science is between The *cosmopolitan democracy* views of Held (1999), Falk (1999) and others, who argue the world is moving towards a new situation within which **supra-national** forms of accountable global governance are being constructed, and *realists* who argue that national political power and associated **international agreements** will continue for the foreseeable future. The *complex multilateralists* **compromise** position of O'Brien et al (2000) suggests that global social movements *do* already influence International Organisations and bypass the national policy making process but national policies are *also* important.

Of course, the political debate about globalisation is not just about whether it is happening or not and the extent to which it is transforming the way the world is governed: it is also about **the form** that globalisation is taking. It is the neo-liberal form of recent globalisation that is often at stake in the globalisation and anti-globalisation debates. Some would be happy to support a globalisation with rules and attention to global social needs.

Held and McGrew (2002) usefully summarise the range of political positions to be found on globalisation which reflect the debate on whether globalisation is really changing things or not and also the form that it is and should be taking. They elaborate a six-fold typology of political positions regarding globalisation.

Three are for globalisation as it is. Neo-liberals celebrate the deregulated global market. Liberal internationalists continue in the tradition of the founders of the UN and see the world as still essentially made up of intergovernmental processes. Institutional reformers make the case for reforming the creaking system of the UN and Bretton Woods. Three positions want to radically mend or abolish globalisation. The global transformers seek to fashion a global world with international social justice and international regulations. On the other hand, Statist/Protectionists believe both that states still matter and want to use them to conserve their country's economic and social achievements against the cold winds of neo-liberal globalisation. Finally, Radicals (which includes both the localists who favour deglobalisation and a nurturing of local resources and the Marxists who may be either for the abolishment of global capitalism but may also be global transformers if they are Marxist social democrats) wish a more fundamental break with capitalist globalisation. They argue that cosmopolitan social democrats can be found occupying the Liberal Internationalist, the Institutional Reforming and the Global Transformer positions. This chapter and the recommendations that flow from it may be regarded as sitting, perhaps uncomfortably, between the Institutional Reforming and the Global Transformation positions.

2.2 Global social policy

Globalisation has affected the way social policy is to be understood and analysed. I have argued elsewhere (Deacon 2000) that globalisation:

- Sets welfare states in competition with each other. This raises the spectre, but not the certainty, of a race to the welfare bottom. It raises the question as to what type of social policy best suits competitiveness without undermining social solidarity.

- Brings new players into the making of Social Policy. International organisations such as the IMF, World Bank, WTO and UN agencies such as WHO and ILO have become involved in prescribing country policy. Also relevant are regional organisations such as MERCOSUR, ASEAN and SADC. International NGOs have substituted for government in this context.

- Generates a global discourse about best social policy. Because supranational actors have become involved, the traditional within-country politics of welfare have taken on a global dimension with a struggle of ideas being waged within and between International Organisations as to desirable social policy. The battle for pension policy in post-communist countries between the World Bank and the ILO was a classic example. (Deacon 1997)

- Creates a global private market in social provision. Increased free trade has created the possibility of mainly USA and European private health care and hospital providers, education providers, social care agencies and social insurance companies benefiting from an international middle-class market in private social provision.

At the same time, globalisation ushers in an era where social policy issues have themselves become globalised. Social policy is, in essence, interventions by governments and other agencies altering the distributive outcomes of market activities. Social policy historically has been about interventions of a socially redistributive kind (from rich to poor, young to old), of a social regulatory kind (setting the social ground rules of a market economy) and of a social rights kind (delimiting the rights and duties of citizens with regard to access to services and incomes). Increased global interconnectedness has globalised these policy issues. Redistribution across borders, social regulations across borders and entitlement to social rights regardless of borders are the global social policy questions needing to be addressed. To put this another way, globalisation is rendering this territorial basis of citizenship obsolete. Identities are increasingly cross border and solidarities arise as much within confessional groupings and ethnicities as within secular states. This raises the issue of international citizenship rights, entitlements and duties.

The field of global social policy may therefore be defined as embracing issues of global redistribution, global regulation and global social rights as shaped by inter-governmental and non-governmental organisations, agencies and groups. The definition also embraces the ways in which such trans-national agencies seek to influence national policy. The governance of global social policy concerns, therefore, the way in which the UN and Bretton Woods institutions and other supranational actors are fashioning both a global social policy in the fields of social protection, education, health and habitat and are influencing national social policies in these fields.

2.3 Global social governance

Whereas within single countries, and even within the most advanced regional grouping of countries (the EU), there are established governance mechanisms and institutions for the formulation and execution of national and regional social policy, this is not the case for the world as a whole. The United Nations system was conceived in an era of inter-nationalisation (not globalisation) and is designed primarily to facilitate country-to-country co-operation. Alongside that have emerged the Bretton Woods organisations that are formally part of the UN system but actually, more often than not, in competition with it. In addition, there are a bewildering array of international civil society actors seeking to influence global policy. At the same time other exclusive groups of countries such as the G7/8 assume authority to make major global social policy initiatives such as forging agreement with international companies to reduce the price of drugs for poor countries.

This chapter and this volume seeks to shed some light on this patchwork of agencies, networks and institutions and the complex ways in which they influence aspects of international social policy. In that sense, the chapter and volume takes the *complex multilateralist* framework as its analytical starting point. Governments still play a major part, but so do trans-border civil society actors interacting with trans-border corporations and international organisations. This work does not undertake a systematic review of all the component parts of this complex whole. We do not, for example, critically review the governance mechanism of the ILO or World Bank in any detail. **What we are trying to capture is something of the ways in which, in the spaces within and between these overlapping and competing agencies, something that passes for a** global governance mechanism, initiating and implementing something that passes for a global social policy, is emerging. At the same time we are arguing that this governance space and this policy is contested. Crucially we are trying to suggest ways in which primarily Northern reform minded governments might intervene in this contested terrain to nudge the world towards a more rules-based international social policy that has equity within and between countries as one of its goals.

3. Global social governance reform issues

As was suggested above, what passes for a system of global governance in the social sphere is a complex of overlapping and competing agencies all seeking to influence policy. There are four areas upon which reform of this global governance 'system' centres:

A. Institutional fragmentation and competition at the global level.
B. The definition of and financing of global public goods.
C. The extent of and mechanisms of global social regulation.
D. The definitions and enforcement of global social rights.

3.1 Institutional fragmentation and competition

At the global level, there are a number of competing and overlapping institutions and groupings of countries, all of which have some stake in shaping global social policy towards global social problems. This struggle for the right to shape policy and for the content of that policy is what passes for an effective system of international social governance. The fragmentation and competition may be analysed as being made up of five groupings of contestations. First, the World Bank, IMF and WTO are in competition for influence with the rest of the UN system. The Bank's health, social protection and education policy for countries is, for example, not the same as that of the WHO, ILO or UNESCO respectively. While the world may be said to have one emerging Ministry of Finance (with lots of shortcoming), it has two Ministries of Health, two Ministries of Social Security and two Ministries of Education. Then again, the UN social agencies (WHO, ILO and UNICEF) do not always espouse the same policy as the UN Department of Economic and Social affairs while the UN Secretary-General's initiatives such as the Global Compact or the Millennium Project may bypass and sideline the social development policies of the UN's Department of Economic and Social affairs. Quite apart from conflicts between the UN and World Bank and within the UN system, there is also the G7, G20, G16, G77 and other groupings of countries. While the rich G7/8 continue to assume the right make global policy, the newer G20 is struggling to forge a broader global consensus and the G77 remains more a party of opposition to the Northern agendas. Regional groupings of countries then have to be brought into the picture. Interaction between these has led to UN international social policy-making in recent years becoming stalemated as the EU, G77 and USA adopt entrenched positions. Bypassing all of this are the ad hoc international initiatives such as the 'Marshall Plans' for Africa, Afghanistan and the Balkans. These are worthy initiatives which are not systematically followed through and funding pledges evaporate when the international spotlight has moved on, while the alternative of independent funding for the UN system which might make follow up more reliable is firmly resisted by the global super-power.

3.2 International finance for global public goods

The increased recognition of and attention to cross border social problems such as disease transmission, illegal economic migration and international drug running has lead to the tabling of the idea of global public goods on the international agenda. A recognition exists that there may be global public goods that need to be provided from which all would benefit but that no particular country or corporation has an interest in providing. The paradox is that this increased recognition coincides with the historic decline of the means of funding such goods (donor AID). Among the policy issues associated with the global public good debate is the definition itself of global public goods. While economists contributing to the debate retain a strict technical definition of public goods, others would extend the definition in terms of what they regard as desirable international public provision. What is desirable then becomes contested. Elsewhere (Deacon 2000), I have criticised the adequacy of the international development targets; the Millennium goals that the OECD, UN and Bank have signed up to in the name of desirable public goods. While basic education for all and clean water should be priority goals, estimates of the costs of meeting them exceed donor commitments. At the same time, attention to the international public funding of basic services only detracts attention from the increased global privatisation of secondary and tertiary education, health and social protection which, if allowed to flourish, will undermine within–country social contracts where all classes have a stake in universal public provision. Regardless of what might be desirable as a shopping list of services that the international community should fund is the inadequacy of international funding mechanisms. The perpetuation (actually decline) of patronising and self interested ODA instead of new forms of international finance is the reality in 2002. Despite the long process leading to the 2002 Monterrey UN Finance for Development Conference, the UN is still struggling to maintain an authority to even consider innovative forms of international financing. At the same time, however, there are moves within the OECD and elsewhere to outlaw tax havens. Progress within the OECD to name and shame tax havens is making some progress in the light of September 11[th,] but any moves to standardise tax rates to combat tax competition, even within the EU, are firmly resisted by some. Instead of new systematic and reliable forms of international finance that would ensure that some global social problems were tackled seriously, we have the emergence of global public-private partnerships such as the GAVI and the Global Fund for AIDS/TB/Malaria (*see* Eeva Ollila's chapter on global health-related public-private partnerships and the United Nations). In the absence of other systematic international funding, these new partnerships and funds attempt to fill the gap but are themselves open to the same donor-pledging shortfall and to the additional criticism that the governing bodies are unaccountable to the UN system and policy.

3.3 Global social regulation

Global or international social policy embraces issues of international social redistribution (discussed in the last section), global social regulation (addressed here) and the enhancement of global social rights (explored in the subsequent section). While fundamentalist neo-liberals see no need for the regulation of the international economy, those who do perceive this need are confronted with a number of seemingly intractable international policy stalemates. Among the current global social regulation issues is the question of how to preserve and improve global labour standards. While the most extreme expressions of Northern protectionism articulated at the 1996 WTO Ministerial Conference have given way to a more nuanced approach on the part of the EU, there is still a North-South impasse between those reformists in the North who would legislate globally now to outlaw 'unacceptable' labour standards and those in the South who argue that such improvement will arise only out of a struggle yet to be fought in the South in the context of development. In the meantime, new ILO core labour standards seem the basis of some interim global consensus. Caught up in the same North-South impasse was the attempt to establish a global set of social policy principles. This worthy idea, articulated first by the UK finance minister Gordon Brown, fell foul of the understandable Southern suspicion that such standards would be used as a new set of social conditionalities imposed on the South while the North still failed to fund their realisation in practice. Of equal importance in this category of global social regulation is the need to regulate emerging international markets in private health, education and social protection. The case for international regulation of these new international providers is only now being articulated. How equitable access to these service providers might be secured is even further down the agenda. Finally, within this category may be put the fraught issue of whether and how to establish voluntary or mandatory guidelines for corporate social responsibility. Attempts to ensure Corporate Social Responsibility are currently focussed on the usefulness of the OECD's guidelines on Multinational Enterprises and the extent to which the UN's Global Compact will actually change business behaviour or merely change business images.

3.4 Global social rights

Citizenship claims have historically been articulated within confined borders and addressed to territorial entities. Globalisation is rendering this territorial basis of citizenship obsolete. Identities are increasingly cross border and solidarities arise as much within confessional groupings and ethnicities as within secular states. This raises the issue of international citizenship rights, entitlements and duties. Among the issues here are the moves to strengthen the attention given to social rights within the UN's international rights agenda and procedures. The UN Secretary-General is proposing one annual country report to the High Commissioner for Human Rights that will cover the full range of international human rights treaties to which they are a party. At the same time, there is a tension between this trajectory of reform and the increased attention being given to cultural and regional diversity. A sharpening of the dissent expressed by some Islamic countries and the Vatican to established UN Human Social and Cultural Rights suggests that the fudged compromises on some of these questions at UN conferences is under pressure. At the same time, the implications of international labour mobility (both legal and illegal) for the social rights of migrants needs considering. The call for dual-citizenship rights for migrant workers is one expression of this. In the same policy terrain are the moves to establish an international social security and social assistance regime. Innovative work on universal socio-economic security within the ILO is breaking from the prior work-based systems of social protection to a citizenship or resident basis of social protection. While there has been some progress in bringing global social rights onto the international agenda, the World Bank until now has avoided using such a concept. But the World Bank has recently set up a working group to evolve its own approach to human rights.

4. Global social governance players and forums

One of the complications of the global social governance reform issue is the large number of forums where agenda setting, policy debates and opinion formation take place. Among these are the Boards of the World Bank and IMF, the joint Bank/IMF Development Committee, and the IMF's International Monetary and Financial

Committee. In addition are the Annual Assemblies and periodic Ministerial meetings of the UN Social agencies (ILO, WHO and UNESCO) as well as the WTO. To these must be added the ad hoc reports to the UN Secretary-General, UN DESA, and UN agencies on aspects of globalisation. Among the most recent and important of these is the WHO Commission on Macroeconomics and Health that reported in December 2001. Upcoming is the ILO's World Commission to examine the Social Dimension of Globalisation. More regularly are the UN ECOSOC meetings together with the UN Commissions on Social Development and on Sustainable Development. These have been punctuated in recent years by the several UN Summits on aspects of social development culminating from the standpoint of global social policy in the Copenhagen and Copenhagen+5 process which concluded in Geneva in 2000.

To this complexity must be added the annual gatherings and working parties of several global think tanks and development networks. Among these are the 'Davos' World Economic Forum, the 'Porto Alegre' World Social Forum, the State of the World Forum's Commission on Globalisation, the Global Development Net (GDN) initially sponsored by the World Bank, and the work of several international philanthropic foundations including the Ford, Rockefeller, Soros, Turner and Gates foundations. Also contributing to the babble of voices are the policy pronouncements of the major international NGOs and civil society organisations including Oxfam, the International Council on Social Welfare (ICSW), Transnational Institute (TNI) and International Confederation of Free Trade Unions (ICFTU)and Southern equivalents such as Third World Network (TWN) and Focus on the Global South. Then again is the work of the OECD, and in particular its recent activities on tax havens, globalisation and development together with its series of regional global forums. At a regional level, there are the meetings of the Trade, Development, Social Affairs, External Affairs, and Enlargement Councils of the European Commission and other regional groupings of countries. Alongside these are the meetings of G7/8, G20, G16 and G77 policy-making processes in international political alliances such as the Second International, and finally international scholarly gatherings and invisible college processes often allied to agenda setting activities such as Stiglitz's Centre for Global Policy alternatives at New York's Colombia University.

Substantive proposals to reform the institutions of global social governance and strong arguments to reform global social policy have emerged from all of these forums. We will consider the substance of some of the more radical of these in the next section. The subsequent section then assesses their viability. Following this, the new form of policy-making process emerging out of this cacophony of stakeholders and voices is discussed.

5. Ambitious global social governance reform

There have been a number of calls for global institutional reform and global social policy change in the past decade from international civil society and scholarly communities. These have included:

- the establishment of a global tax authority;
- the expansion of the G20 to include regional groups of countries;
- the further democratisation of the UN by means of a world peoples' assembly;
- mechanisms to make the Bretton Woods institutions more accountable to those who receive loans;
- the creation of an Economic Security Council.

A range of recent international reports and publications were reviewed to form a basis for points made in this chapter[1]. Taken as representative of what it is acceptable to place on the international policy agenda by those engaged directly in nudging reform forward, it can be seen that some of these reforms do find a place. UN democratisation and better inter agency co-operation is there. Greater accountability of the Bretton Woods institutions figures also. A strengthened ECOSOC crops up several times. Global taxation is, however, something that is felt to be difficult to defend against the world super-power. At the same time, some of the reports point in the direction of some of the newer global governance mechanisms which are discussed in a later section of this chapter, namely Global Policy Networks.

In terms of recommendations from the scholarly community, we should include a major review of the World Bank and the UN, *Dinosaurs or Dynamos* by Bergensen and Lunde (1999), who concluded that the UN should retreat to fulfilling a normative function – setting guidelines and rules and doing this well – and should leave the Bank to implement development practice. It did, however, suggest that the Bank could alternatively aim to be the global repository of knowledge on development questions. This would, I believe, continue the constant tension between the UN and the Bank, both competing to define good policy and practice with different ideological slants.

Two more recent books writing within this formal approach to global institutional change and to the reform of global social policy are those by Nayyar and Townsend.

---

[1] Reviewed were the UNDP Human Development Report 2002 which addressed issue of global democracy; the Outcome of the UN's 2002 Finance for Development Conference; the Copenhagen+5 final report from 2000; the recent WHO Report of the Macro-Economic Commission; and the Millennium Report of the Secretary-General. The table produced is available from the Author.

Deepak Nayyar (2002) in *Governing Globalisation* calls for three institutional changes in the sphere of social policy: a) full or partial independent UN funding, b) the establishment of a Global Peoples Assembly, and c) the creation of an Economic Security Council to parallel the Security Council. This Council would ensure that the United Nations provides an institutional mechanism for consultation on global economic policies.

In terms of global social policy, Townsend (2002) has published a manifesto for international action to defeat poverty which makes 18 points such as the global legal enforcement of a right to an adequate standard of living, the global legal requirement on all developed countries to contribute 1% of GNP to overseas development and the introduction of new international company law. We return in the next section to the political viability of the implementation of such reforms and to whether it is appropriate any longer to think in terms of such major institutional change and major policy shifts.

One way of imagining an even more radical global social governance reform is to project onto the global level those institutions and policies in the social sphere that operate at national and regional (EU) level. In the first table, we can see how far we are from establishing at a global level anything approaching a system of social governance that is already emerging at the European level. In the second table, we can see what kind of institutional reform would be required at the global level to emulate national and European governance and policy-making.

Table A. The social functions of governance at national, regional and global level

FUNCTION/ POLICY FIELD	NATIONAL GOVERNMENT	EU REGIONAL GOVERNMENT	CURRENT GLOBAL ARRANGEMENTS
Economic stability	Central Banks	Central Bank in EURO zone Settlements?	IMF/ Bank of International
Revenue Raising	National taxation	Customs revenues plus government 'donations' (talk of tax harmony and regional tax)	None but mix of UN appeals, ad hoc global funds, bi and multilateral ODA.
Redistribution	Tax and income transfers policy plus regional funds	Structural funds on social criteria.	None but ad hoc humanitarian relief, special global funds, debt relief and differential pricing (drugs).
Social Regulation (Labour and social standards)	State laws and directives.	EU laws and directives.	Soft ILO, WHO etc conventions. UN Conventions. Voluntary codes.
Social Rights (Citizenship Empowerment)	Court redress. Consumer charters. Tripartite governance.	EU Luxembourg Court Redress. Tripartite Governance.	UN Commission For Human Rights but no legal redress. Civil Society Monitoring.

Table B. The current institutions of social governance at national and EU level and suggested reformed institutions at the global level

CONSTITUENT INTERESTS	NATIONAL INSTITUTIONS	EU REGIONAL INSTITUTIONS	POTENTIAL REFORMED GLOBAL INSTITUTIONS
The electorate	Parliament.	EU Parliament with fewer powers	World Peoples Assembly?
Government Ministers	Cabinet etc.	Councils of Ministers	Reformed UN ECOSOC?
Civil Service	Ministries.	EU Commission	Combination and Rationalisation of Overlapping Sector Functions of UNDESA, UNDP, ILO, WHO, UNESCO, World Bank, WTO, OECD, and NEW Tax Authority.
Judiciary	Courts	Luxembourg Court (And C of E Strasbourg Court of Human Rights)	New International Court with Human Rights Mandate.
Capital	Central Bank	Central Bank	Central Bank
Labour (civil society)	Trade Unions (TUs) and statutory consultations.	TUs on Economic and Social Committee and consultations.	Enhanced TU and civil society consultation mechanisms

To make this suggestion that we might model a reformed global governance on EU governance mechanisms is not to endorse uncritically as fully effective these EU mechanisms. Indeed, as I have argued elsewhere (Deacon 1999), the response of the EU to neo-liberal globalisation in terms of both its internal and external social dimension has been variable over time and between component parts of the EU system. The EU has not consistently been a model for a transformed socially responsible globalisation. The EU has exhibited tendencies to:

- accommodation to the liberalising global agenda in labour markets and associated social policy;
- social protectionist inclinations in some of its trade dealings;
- ineffectiveness in terms of World Bank discussions on global financial regulation.

Its parliament has limited powers, the Union has yet to enshrine its policy on human and social rights into law, the effectiveness of its social fund is questioned and it possesses no independent taxation authority.

While ambitious reformist ideas of this kind may be regarded as utopian at best, it is to be noted that some of these issues do surface in the latest Report of the Secretary-General to the 57th session of the UN which is entitled *Strengthening of the United Nations: an agenda for further change.* It recognises (para.19) the growing role of the UN in helping to forge consensus on globally important social and economic issues and calls for the corresponding strengthening of the principal organ concerned with those issues, namely the Economic and Social Council (ECOSOC). It stresses the need for improved agendas and stream-lined business. At the same time, the report (para.130) says the Department of Economic and Social Affairs will be strengthened with the appointment of a new Assistant General Secretary and the creation of a policy-planning unit within it.

6. Obstacles to ambitious global social governance reform and likely pragmatic developments

In practice, of course, there are many political and institutional obstacles to such radical reforms as the merging of the Bank and the UN agencies into one global civil service, and creating a new source of UN funding. Even the attempt to make the ECOSOC an effective body that would be taken seriously by the Bank and the US government is harder than the UN Secretary-General might imagine. Only the high level segment of ECOSOC brings together Ministers who have these issues as their brief. More often, lower level meetings are bedevilled by the basic problem that besets most UN meetings, the inability of the country delegate to address the substantive issues at hand. Ill worked out country positions on social and economic agenda items are conveyed by civil servants whose expertise does not lie in this area. While countries do not have a coherent and joined-up policy towards global economic and social issues such that each Ministry and hence each UN delegate speaks to the same brief, it is impossible to expect ECOSOC to evolve through debate a coherent global economic and social policy. At the same time, ECOSOC is structured such that the Second Committee considers economic matters and the Third Committee considers social matters, further preventing the development of a coherent UN economic and social policy. Quite apart from the unworkable political process flowing from the flawed UN concept of one nation one vote, even getting a coherent global economic and social policy within the Executive of the UN is problematic. For example, the Department of Social Policy Development did not collaborate with the upstairs Division for Public Economics and Public Administration (PEPA) on the PEPA's new volume on *The World Public Sector Report: Globalization and the State* (2002).

This in-house fragmentation is, of course, why the Secretary-General is proposing a strengthened policy unit inside the Department of Economic and Social Affairs. In the meantime, he is in effect creating his own UN Economic and Social Policy that emerges in practice through the networked processes of the Global Compact and the Millennium Project and bypasses those charged within UNDESA to fashion such a policy in dialogue with country delegates in ECOSOC and the Commission on Social Development.

But the obstacles to such major institutional reforms or such mould-breaking global policy initiatives are greater than these. They include Southern resistance to the Northern reform agenda favouring de-globalisation. A number of writers from the South have pointed out that the history of Northern imposed conditions in the context of structural adjustment means that even well-intentioned Northern reform ideas are unlikely to be received readily (www.focusweb.org), (www.global-South.net), (www.undp.org/tscd). As we have seen, reaction against the worst excesses of global neo-liberalism gave rise in the 1990s to a number of mainly Northern generated initiatives to begin to challenge this policy drift, to reinsert a social purpose into the global economy and to counter some of the more obvious negative aspects of partial global economic integration. These included the suggestion to include a social clause in trade agreements; the proposition for a better-than-safety-net set of global social policy principles; the emergence of the discourse concerning global public goods; the increased emphasis given to social rights in the human rights agenda; and the emergence onto the UN agenda of global tax regulation. But in terms of reaching a North-South agreement on a global approach to national social policy that goes beyond safety nets, there are real obstacles to be overcome. An impasse now seems to have been reached in the global dialogue concerning desirable social policies to be implemented in an era of globalisation. Northern-based global social reform initiatives, such as the social policies principles initiative, that were concerned to modify the free play of global market forces with appropriate global social policies of international regulation have met with understandable but frustrating opposition from many Southern governments and some Southern-based NGOs and social movements. The debate in Geneva 2000 characterized this development when the proposal for a set of social policy principles was rejected on the grounds that these might become a new conditionality imposed by the North and that there was anyway no money forthcoming from the richer countries to help pay for the implementation of such principles. Moves beyond this impasse would seem to require two changes. One would be a greater commitment on the part of the North to support international resource transfers to pay for global public goods such as basic universal education combined with an opening of trade opportunities in the North for Southern countries. The other is for the South to own and develop for itself any such social policy principles or standards based on a review of best practice in the South.

At the same time, there has emerged the very important Northern 'neo-liberalism' alliance with this Southern resistance that in part champions global neo-liberalism and unfettered increased free trade as being in the interests of the South. The UK, in criticising some of the EU and the USA's worst policies of protectionism, are champions of Southern empowerment and development through trade (www.dfid.gov.uk). This is potentially a powerful North-South alliance that might challenge other North-South alliances that are more concerned to establish global social ground rules and effective global social institutions. But government ministers Gordon Brown and Clare Short, as central actors in this UK strategy, do also address the issue of global inequity. They initiated the stalled global social policy principles, pursued the reduction of drug prices for Southern countries, and are among the most articulate global players supporting the need for more finance for achieving the international development goals. Any serious attempt to build an alternative global political alliance for more systematic global social policy reform needs to engage them. (*See* Brown, *A New Deal for the World*, www.fabianglobalforum.net).

Finally, as a further obstacle to ambitious global social governance reform is the continued appeal of national sovereignty combined with a limited popular constituency for radical global reform. This and the appeal of cultural diversity will ensure that any attempt to construct a more effective system of international governance will meet with resistance. The national basis of democratic process feeds this conservatism. Unless the global reform agenda also addresses the case for a culturally pluralist world, progress will be limited.

All of this suggests, therefore, that a reform agenda that is more circumscribed than Ambitious Reformism is the likely prospect for the next decade. This might embody elements of moves to a constructive regionalism with a social dimension as a building block to an inter-regional globalisation that acknowledges the case for pluralism. The problem is that, in some parts of the world, regional groupings of countries are underdeveloped. We may also expect increased International Institutional Cooperation and Policy Convergence rather than a realignment of power between the World Bank and UN. On the feasible agenda is funding and mechanisms to facilitate a more effective Southern voice(s) in the global debates and institutions such as the WTO. We will see more Global 'Philanthropy', donation and public-private partnerships rather than global taxation, and probably the improvement of the UN's Global Compact with an element of monitoring and including voluntary regulation to encourage 'socially responsible' TNCs. Certainly, there will be more tasks forces and ad hoc initiatives of the Millennium Project kind, demonstrating in practice how global social policy change might be forged.

This is not to dismiss some of these steps as unhelpful from the standpoint of the wider agenda to reform neo-liberal globalisation. In particular, the moves to constructive regionalism with a social dimension and the increasing empowerment of some Southern countries in the global arena is to be welcomed.

Several emerging trading blocs and other regional associations of countries in the South are beginning to confront in practice the issues of the relationship between trade and labour, social and health standards, and the issue of how to maintain levels of taxation in the face of competition to attract capital. In this context, the potential advantages for developing countries of building a social dimension to regional groupings of countries are being considered. Such advantages may be summarised as having an external and internal dimension. In relation to the rest of the world, such an approach affords protection from global market forces that might erode national social entitlements and can create the possibility of such grouped countries having a louder voice in the global discourse on economic and social policy in UN and other fora. Internally, through intergovernmental agreement, regionalism would make possible the development of regional social redistribution mechanisms, regional social and labour regulations and regional sectoral social policies in health and education. They might also develop regional social empowerment mechanisms that give citizens a voice to challenge their governments in terms of supranational human and social rights. A regional approach could facilitate intergovernmental co-operation in social policy in terms of regional health specialization, regional education cooperation, regional food and livelihood cooperation, and regional recognition of social security entitlements. This in turn would facilitate the regulation of the de-facto private regional social policies of health, education and social protection companies.

7. Global networks, partnerships and projects, or global political alliances?

Because significant global institutional reform seems check-mated and major global social policy change is difficult to achieve, and because there are now so many loci of action and initiatives on global social issues, **we may be witnessing a shift in the *locus* and *content* of policy debate and activity from those more formally located within the official UN policy making arenas (whether of ECOSOC in New York or in the councils of the ILO and WHO in Geneva) and focussed on UN/Bretton Woods institutional reform such as the establishment of an Economic Security Council to a set of practices around Networks, Partnerships and Projects which, in some ways bypass, these institutions and debates and present new possibilities for actually making global change in particular social policy arenas.**

Ngaire Woods, in a chapter in Held and McGrew's (2002) *Governing Globalisation*, argues:

"The global governance debate is focused heavily on the reform and creation of international institutions....yet global governance is increasingly being undertaken by a variety of networks, coalitions and informal arrangements which lie a little further beyond the public gaze and the direct control of governments. *It is these forms of governance that need sustained and focussed attention to bring to light whose interests they further and to whom they are accountable.* (emphasis added)

Among examples of these networks, partnerships and projects are the UN Secretary-General's Millennium Project involving ten task forces to manage the implementation of the Millennium Development Goals. The essence of this emerging networking and partnership form of policy development and practice-shifting through a focus on specific projects is the collaboration between stakeholders in international organisations, the global corporate sector, international NGOs and civil society organisations. Such a shift in the locus and substance of global policy-making and practice has received support recently from commentators coming from very different intellectual positions. Rischard (2002), The World Bank's Vice President for Europe, in *High Noon: 20 Global Issues and 20 Years to Solve Them,* argues that global multilateral institutions are not able to handle global issues on their own, that treaties and conventions are too slow for burning issues, that intergovernmental conferences do not have adequate follow up mechanisms and that the G7/8 type groupings are too exclusive. Instead, what is needed are Global Issues Networks (GINs) involving governments, civil society and business facilitated by a lead multilateral organisation which create a rough consensus about the problem to be solved and the task to be achieved, the norms to be established and the practice recommendations and which then report on failing governments and encourage good practice through knowledge exchange and a global observatory which feeds a name-and-shame approach. Charlotte Streck in *Global Environmental Governance: Options and Opportunities* argues for Global Public Policy Networks (GPPNs) which bring together governments, the private sector and civil society organisations. She insists that recent trends in international governance indicate that the focus has shifted from intergovernmental activity to multi-sectoral initiatives from a largely formal legalistic approach to a less formal participatory and integrated approach. Such GPPNs can agenda-set, standard-set, generate and disseminate knowledge and bolster institutional effectiveness. Streck is building here on the work of Reinicke and Bennet (2000) who argued that International Organisations had a particular role they could play in GPPNs as convenor, platform, net-worker and sometimes partial financier (*see also* www.gppi.net).

There is clearly something in these accounts of the way policy-making has become projectised and task centred. A key question is how intervention in these tasks and projects might be anything other than opportunistic or self interested or pragmatic. Because so much of this kind of work is subcontracted in terms of its intellectual and policy content and in terms of implementation, principles that guide these actors become important. This raises the question again of how these principles are to come into being. There is a case, therefore, for not only the networks and partnerships focused on short-term projects and tasks but also for longer term *global political alliances* that might fashion sets of principles and steer members of the task forces. If intervention to mend neo-liberal globalisation is project based, then the actors in those projects need a solid ethical reference point and set of policy principles against which they can assess their proposals for action. We are back to global social policy, but not a policy to be debated and won in the chambers of the UN or won in intellectual dialogue with Bank experts (though these activities need to continue): instead, a policy implemented in practice by those who find themselves on such projects. A global reformist political alliance would act as a reference point for actors in practice.

Attempts to forge such global policy frameworks to guide practice exist. The Second Socialist International is one such mechanism which fosters a common approach to international policy issues in all countries which are run by parties affiliated to it but is becoming less effective as power shifts from governments to networks. A novel alternative is the International Simultaneous Policy Organisation (ISPO) (www.simpol.org) which attempts to foster a common policy agenda such as the Tobin Tax in all governments at the same time but, again, it is government focussed. Some global foundations have turned recently to global policy advocacy in an attempt to shift international practice. Rockefeller has a Global Inclusion Project. Carnegie within the framework of its Global Policy Programme has set up a Managing Global Issues Project to learn lessons within a value framework from attempts to solve different global problems. Stiglitz is encouraging reflection upon such issues within his new Centre for Policy Alternatives. The Helsinki Conference for Democracy and Globalisation might be another such seeking 'Transformative Global Partnerships' (www.helsinkiconference.fi).

There are three kinds of already existing global political alliances that need to be taken into account in shaping what I am now arguing for. There is the global civil society alliance based on the Porte Allegro process. While this is a rich mix of organisations and interests, it is stumbling towards articulating an alternative globalisation. At the same time, the major thrust of the UN Secretary-General and some of the UN agencies at the moment seems to be toward cementing the global UN-business alliance. What is missing is global political alliance for a reformed globalisation that is centred upon reform-minded governments and reform-minded international civil servants. In its place is the other actually existing global political alliance described earlier. The UK-led North-South alliance for Southern involvement in the global economy fleshed out with ad-hoc initiatives such as support for the Millennium targets and reduced drug prices occupies this space. Space exists for a coalition to be formed of like–minded governments together with actors within the UN system and some major INGOs to work towards the articulation of a globalisation with rules and justice governed by a more coherent global governance system. Work within the Second International could form a basis of this but the coalition needs to be much broader. Those who share this perspective and who are in a position to influence the direction of the G20 or have the opportunity to work to reform ECOSOC or who are able to influence the IMF/World Bank Development Committee or who are able to shape the outcome of the World Commission on the Social Dimension of Globalisation or are otherwise influential on the global policy stage need to address concrete policy options for improved global social governance. Is the call for an Economic Security Council viable or is reform of ECOSOC a better bet? Can USA objection to global taxation ever be overcome/bypassed and how? Is activity targeted at improving global governance misguided and effort better expended within each region to construct a decentred globalisation of constructive regionalism? At the same time, such a global political alliance could articulate principles for practice within the new governance modes of networks, projects and partnerships. If Global Policy Networks are the way forward and, as the Secretary-General says in his Millenium Report "need a more focused and systematic approach", then such a global political alliance could be a systematic policy reference point for those engaged in such networks.

8. A Strategy for Finland and like-minded countries

The Report on Globalisation of the Ministry of Foreign Affairs of Finland to the Foreign Affairs Committee of Parliament in 2001 stated "Finland supports the development of the UN as the principal actor in the democratic management of globalisation". Finland "aims at managing globalisation by developing more comprehensive and effective mechanisms and rules for international cooperation". Some other like-minded countries have begun to articulate similar globalisation policies.

It might be hoped that Finnish and like-minded government policy on Global Social Governance will develop towards a more comprehensive and radical policy that embraces some elements of the radical social governance reform agenda described earlier. Thus it might aim for:

1. A more equitable globalisation;
2. A more socially regulated globalisation;
3. A more powerful role for the UN in global economic and social affairs;
4. The introduction of new international taxation to pay for global public goods.
5. The empowerment of the South in international decision-making processes.

At the same time, such countries need to engage with the more limited viable reform agenda described earlier and will be engaged in networks, partnerships and projects seeking to change international practice. Among the tactics and strategies available to the Finnish and like-minded governments for furthering both the more ambitious reform agenda and for helping to ensure that project practice is governed by principle rather than just pragmatism might be the following:

1. Working within the EU to strengthen its voice as a 'progressive' global player in these policy discussions in several forums and work within other regions to argue for the replication of EU practices where appropriate.

2. Collaborating via the EU with the G77 to secure a greater EU – South understanding on global governance issues.

3. Increasing funding opportunities for South-South collaboration and Southern empowerment in the international governance system.

4. Utilising the placement of Finnish civil servants and experts in secondments to International Organisations and Task forces to spread by soft-means-best social policy practice.

5. Working to strengthen those actors in the UN system who are finding ways of applying the Nordic traditions of equity and universalism on an international scale (UNRISD, UNICEF and ILO-SES).

6. Maximising the impact of the Finnish joint Presidency of the ILO World Commission by engaging directly on the global political stage with other key national players such as the UK who are adopting a more neo-liberal global agenda.

7. Utilising the current Finnish membership of the ECOSOC Board in conjunction with new and subsequent President of ECOSOC to work quietly for the strengthening of the role of a reformed ECOSOC in the global management of the economy.

8. Work with like-minded countries such as Canada to give greater credence to the role of the G20 and especially argue for its potential for being a world economic authority that involves Southern regional blocs as members.

9. Encourage Finnish based business to lead the way in accepting the importance of international social regulations rather than weaker international voluntary agreements.

10. Encourage (maybe after the ILO Commission has reported) the regular meetings of like-minded national and international actors who favour a reformed globalisation. One possibility is working to build upon the regular UNRISD retreats of UN Social Agencies and argue to expand these to include individuals in the World Bank, WTO as well as other key sympathetic global players such as those in the G20 and G77 in order to construct a global political intergovernmental alliance for global social governance reform. This intergovernmental and IO alliance would compliment and work with emerging international NGO/ civil society alliances such as the Porto Alegre process. It would be a global reformist policy alliance. It would be a complement to the UN's compact with the business world. The Helsinki conference process is a possible starting point for such a global social reformist political alliance

From the earlier analysis, four principles may be drawn out to guide the policy and practice of Finland and like-minded countries as they engage in the kinds of activities listed above:

- **Forging alliances with global Southern country partners and groups within which Southern voices are heard.** Empowering developing countries in international forums should be a priority for Northern governments.
- **Supporting approaches to world regionalism within which the social dimension of trading arrangements is given due attention.** This way an alternative to global neo-liberalism can be built.
- **Working always to achieve a more equitable access to services and provision** both within and between countries.
- **Establishing within-country policy synergy towards global questions across all Ministries.** Contributing to an equitable and ruled based globalisation must become lenses through which all government policy is filtered. This point is developed below.

Key is within country synergy on a progressive approach to globalisation.

We conclude by insisting that, in order to secure a more effective role within the global governance reform debate and practice, a requirement is that *all* Finnish

Ministries and government agencies, (and to a lesser extent Finnish business and civil society) act with a *common policy on globalisation* that is guided by the equitable and rule-based principles suggested earlier. This is a reflection of the point made earlier about the difficulty at the UN level of forging a common consensus and compromise on globalisation policy when countries themselves do not have such a coherent approach.

International equitable and sustainable social development should become not only the policy of the Finnish Development Agency and Finnish Social Policy but also the policy of the Ministry of Trade and the Ministry of Finance.

Policy synergy is the key to effective national action on the global stage. Policy coherence between the UN social agencies and the Bank/WTO/IMF is predicated upon policy coherence between National Ministries of Social and Development Affairs and National Ministries of Finance and Trade and Agriculture.

Ruth Jacoby, Director-General for International Development Co-operation for Sweden and Chair of the UN Conference on Finance for Development in Monterrey, speaking at the ICSW'international conference in June 2002, argued that synergy between the portfolios of national ministries of finance, trade, agriculture and those concerned with social development questions was the key to a better world.

For Finland and other like-minded countries, the priority would seem to be a series of within country inter-Ministerial meetings to ensure a greater degree of policy coherence centred on achieving a progressive role for Finland in the international debates and practices with regard to the social dimension of globalisation. All Ministerial policy of all Ministers needs to be assessed against this benchmark.

Acknowledgements

I would like to thank Minna Ilva for background research that informed this chapter and my other GASPP colleagues, Paul Stubbs, Eeva Ollila and Meri Koivusalo, for comments on earlier versions of this work.

Bob Deacon, November 2002

References

Annan, K. A. (2000), 'We the People's'. The role of United Nations in the 21st century. United Nations, New York.

Bergensen, H. O. and Lunde, L. (1999), *Dinosaurs or Dynamos: The United Nations and The World Bank at the Turn of the Century,* Earthscan, London.

Brown, G. (2002), *A New Deal for the World,* [online] available: www.fabianglobalforum.net/forum/article014.html.

Castells, M. (1996), *The Rise of the Network Society,* Blackwell, Oxford.

Deacon, B. (1999), *Socially Responsible Globalisation: A Challenge for the European Union,* Ministry of Social Affairs and Health, Helsinki.

Deacon, B. (2000), *Globalization and Social Policy,* United Nations Research Institute for Social Development, Geneva.

Deacon, B. (2001), *The Social Dimension of Regionalism,* Stakes, Helsinki.

Deacon, B. (2003) The Prospects for Equitable Access to Social Provision in a Globalizing World, in: Krizsan, A. et al (eds) *Reshaping Globalization: Multilateral Dialogues and New Policy Initiatives,* Central European University Press, Budapest.

Deacon, B., Hulse, M. and Stubbs, P. (1997), *Global Social Policy: international organizations and the future of welfare,* Sage, London.

Falk, R. (1999), Humane governance for the world: Reviving the quest, *Review of International Political Economy,* vol. 7, no. 2, pp. 317–34.

Held, D. and McGrew, A. (2002), *Governing Globalization,* Polity Press, Cambridge.

Held, D., McGrew A. et al (eds.) (1999), *Global Transformations: Politics, Economics and Culture,* CUP, Cambridge.

Ministry for Foreign Affairs of Finland (2001), *A Report on Globalization for the Foreign Affairs Committee of Parliament,* [online] available: www.formin.fi/english/.

Mishra, R. (1999), *Globalization and the Welfare State,* Edward Elgar, Cheltenham.

Nayyar, D. (Ed.) (2002), *Governing Globalization. Issues and Institutions,* Oxford University Press.

O'Brien, R., Goetz, A. M., Scholte, J. A. and William, M. (2000), *Contesting Global Governance: Multilateral Economic Institutions and Global Social Movements,* Cambridge University Press, Cambridge.

Rischard, J. F. (2002), *High Noon: Twenty Global Problems, Twenty Years to Solve Them,* Perseus Books, Oxford.

Scholte, J. A. (2000), *Globalization: A Critical Introduction,* Macmillan, London.

Streck, C. (2002), Global Public Policy Networks as Coalitions for Change, in: Esty, D. and Ivanova, M. H. (eds), *Global Environmental Governance: Options and Opportunities,* Yale University, Yale.

Therborn, G. (2000), Globalization: Dimensions, Historical Waves, Regional Effects, Normative Governance, *International Sociology,* 15.

Townsend, P. and Gordon, D. (eds.) (1999), *World Poverty: New policies to defeat an old enemy,* Policy Press, Bristol.

United Nations (2000), *Further initiatives for social development,* 5 Dec 2000. A/RES/S-24/2.

United Nations (2002) Plan of Implementation of the World Summit on Sustainable Development, in: *Report of the World Summit on Sustainable Development,* Johannesburg, South Africa, 26 Aug – 4 Sep 2002, A/CONF.199/20.

United Nations (2002), *Report of the International Conference on Financing for Development,* A/CONF.198/11.

United Nations (2002), *Strengthening of the United Nations: an agenda for further change,* Report of the Secretary-General, A/57/387/Corr.1.

United Nations (2002), Plan of Implementation of the World Summit on Sustainable Development. In: *Report of the World Summit on Sustainable Development.* Johannesburg, South Africa, 26 Aug – 4 Sep 2002. A/CONF.199/20.

United Nations (2000) *Further intiatives for social development.* Resolution adopted by he General Assembly. 15 Dec 2000. A/RES/S-24/2.

United Nations Development Programme (2002), *Human Development Report 2002. Deepening Democracy in a Fragmented World,* Oxford University Press, New York.

Witte, J. M., Reinicke, W. H. and Bennet, T. (2000) Beyond Multilateralism: Global Public Policy Networks, *International Politics and Society,* 2.

Woods, N. (2002), Global; Governance and the Role of Institutions, in: Held, D. and McGrew, A. (eds), *Governing Globalization,* Polity Press, Cambridge.

World Health Organization (2002), *Macroeconomics and Health: Investing in Health for Economic Development* , [online] available: www.who.int/cmhreport (October 2002)

II
HEALTH-RELATED PUBLIC-PRIVATE PARTNERSHIPS AND THE UNITED NATIONS

Eeva Ollila

Senior Researcher
Globalism and Social Policy Programme (GASPP)
STAKES

1. Introduction

The UN's interactions with business have changed in nature and in volume during the past decade, a change that reflects shifts in the general political and economic environment over this time. Since the beginning of the 1990s, business has been increasingly invited to the UN gatherings, while various forms of interactions between the business community and UN agencies have become more frequent. More recently, major global public-private partnerships to address essential public health issues have been formed, some of which are largely outside the auspices of the UN.

In this paper, the term public-private *interaction* (PPI) is used as a general term for interaction between the UN and for-profit entities. The term public-private *partnership* (PPP) mainly refers to those interactions that include for-profit entities in public-policy making and in setting public agendas and priorities. But as the terms are used very loosely by the UN system itself, some confusion is inevitable.

The objective of this paper is threefold: to trace the development of PPIs between the UN and business in areas related to health; to look at the safeguards (or lack of them) in place to ensure the integrity of the UN; and to articulate the possible risks and problems for the UN in pursuing PPIs. The organizations surveyed in this paper include the World Health Organization (WHO) and the UN's two health-related funds – the United Nations Children's Fund (Unicef) and the United Nations Fund for Population (UNFPA). The World Bank and the joint United Nations Programme on HIV/AIDS (UNAIDS) remain largely outside the scope of this paper. The paper also looks at the Global Compact and several major PPPs dealing with essential public health issues, namely, the Global Alliance for Vaccines Initiative (GAVI), the Global Fund to Fight AIDS, Tuberculosis and Malaria (GFATM), and the Global Alliance for Improved Nutrition (GAIN), which all together are called global health-related public-private partnerships (GHPPP).

The paper starts by looking at development within the general UN framework, WHO and within the two UN health-related funds, Unicef and UNFPA. This section explores the overall mandate given for increased interactions with business and goes on to look at specific examples of collaboration between the UN and business. It looks at definitions of PPPs given by the various UN agencies, the stated expectations of PPPs and the activities related to business interactions within the Global Compact, WHO, Unicef and UNFPA. The paper then looks briefly at governance and the actual content of GHPPPs. It continues to analyse the procedures in place for assessing and selecting PPPs and the potential risks and problems for the UN and for public interests related to PPPs and PPIs. The paper concludes with some recommendations for the Finnish government and like-minded countries.

In addition to literature, this paper is based on interviews and email communications with staff in the various UN agencies and GHPPPs. Those interviewed were from WHO (7 persons), Unicef (9 persons), UNFPA (4 persons), UNAIDS (1 person), Global Compact (1 person), the UN Fund for International Partnerships (UNFIP) (1 person), GAVI (1 person) and GFATM (1 person). Discussions were also held with the Finnish Unicef Association, the Finnish Foreign Ministry and several people who used to work in various UN agencies.

2. Development of the UN's interactions with the private sector

WE THE PEOPLES OF THE UNITED NATIONS DETERMINED

to save succeeding generations from the scourge of war, which twice in our lifetime has brought untold sorrow to mankind, and
to reaffirm faith in fundamental human rights, in the dignity and worth of the human person, in the equal rights of men and women and of nations large and small, and
to establish conditions under which justice and respect for the obligations arising from treaties and other sources of international law can be maintained, and
to promote social progress and better standards of life in larger freedom,

AND FOR THESE ENDS

to practice tolerance and live together in peace with one another as good neighbours, and
to unite our strength to maintain international peace and security, and
to ensure, by the acceptance of principles and the institution of methods, that armed force shall not be used, save in the common interest, and
to employ international machinery for the promotion of the economic and social advancement of all peoples,

HAVE RESOLVED TO COMBINE OUR EFFORTS TO ACCOMPLISH THESE AIMS

Accordingly, our respective Governments, through representatives assembled in the city of San Francisco, who have exhibited their full powers found to be in good and due form, have agreed to the present Charter of the United Nations and do hereby establish an international organization to be known as the United Nations.

Preamble to the UN Charter (1945)

Interactions between the United Nations and the private sector have grown exponentially in recent years, although such interactions are by no means new – in fact, they are as old as the UN Charter itself (Tesner with Kell 2000). The UN has always had extensive commercial links with the private sector through its procurement activities, while the private sector has, at times, participated, directly or indirectly, in the normative and standard-setting work of the UN (Mezzalama and Ouedraogo 1999). But a significant change in the paradigm and in the actual ways and extent to which the UN engages with the corporate sector has taken place within the last decade or so. This development is not only a reflection of changes in the global political and economic environment; it is also a reinforcing force within that development. This increase in interactions with the private sector has not happened by itself. Besides overall political and economic changes, the financial constraints of the UN, as well as the direct pressures that some member states have exerted on the UN to engage more with the private sector have been important in that change.

Some turning points within the broader and subtler changes within the global political and economic environment can be traced back to various events and moments within UN conferences and decisions. Representatives of the business world were invited to attend and to provide inputs into the international UN-sponsored conferences of the 1990s (Mezzalama and Ouedraogo 1999), such as the 1992 UN Conference on Environment and Development (UNCED), dubbed the "Earth Summit" (Tesner with Kell, 2000). In health-related areas, the latter half of the 1990s witnessed an increasing number of initiatives involving collaboration between the corporate and public sectors (Buse and Walt 2000).

In January 1997, meanwhile, just a few weeks after he had been elected Secretary-General of the UN, Kofi Annan gave a speech at the annual World Economic Forum, a gathering of the world business leaders, in Davos, Switzerland, in which he said that the close link between the private sector and the work of the UN was a vitally important one. He called for a new partnership among governments, the private sector and the international community. He said that:

"Strengthening the partnership between the United Nations and the private sector will be one of the priorities of my term as Secretary-General."

(Annan 1997)

Kofi Annan started to apply this new thinking and implement the imperative of change to an ongoing UN reform process (Tesner with Kell 2000, 33). In June 1997 major transnational companies had been invited to a meeting held at the United Nations building to examine steps towards establishing terms of reference for business sector participation in the policy setting processes of the UN and partnering in the uses of UN development funds (Korten 1997). In July 1997, Kofi Annan unveiled a UN reform proposal, which emphasized the role of civil society as not only a disseminator of information or provider of services but also as a shaper of policy. Civil society meant NGOs, academic and research institutions, parliamentarians *and* corporations. The proposal also included suggestions that corporations would play an indirect role in the UN's General Assembly (A/51/950[1]). Maurice Strong, a former CEO of several large corporations and the mastermind of business involvement in the Earth Summit, had chaired the reform process that resulted in this proposal. The proposal provoked many responses, and developing countries in particular expressed caution about the suggestions for increased private sector interactions (Tesner with Kell, 2000, 33–5). But later that same year, the General Assembly "underlined the positive role of the private sector in supporting economic growth and development as well as in the mobilizing of resources" and "called upon the UN funds and programmes […] in their work in implementing the present resolution, to give due consideration to the role of the private sector in development" (A/52/209).

By the time of the World Economic Forum two years later in January 1999, Kofi Annan was ready to call upon the business community to join the UN in a Global Compact, having actively searched in the interim for private sector collaborators. The Compact was an arrangement in which business would embrace nine principles of good conduct in the areas of human rights, labour standards and environmental practices, all areas in which universal values had been defined by international agreements. He said:

"I made the point that the everyday work of the United Nations – whether in peacekeeping, setting technical standards, protecting intellectual property rights or providing much needed assistance to developing countries – helps to expand opportunities for the business around the world." (Annan 1999)

---

[1] Official UN and WHO documents are referred to by their official reference number. They can be found from the web sites of the organisations by this number, except for the provisional summary records from WHO, abbreviated by SR, which can be obtained as printed copies from WHO.

Stressing global markets and the preferential nature of voluntary good conduct over obligatory regulation, he added:

> "I fear that, if we do not act, there may be a threat to the open global market, and especially to the multilateral trade regime. There is enormous pressure from various interest groups to load trade regime and investment agreements with restrictions aimed at preserving standards in the three areas I have just mentioned. These are legitimate concerns. But restrictions on trade and investment are not the right means to use when tackling them. Instead, we should find a way to achieve our proclaimed standards by other means. And that is precisely what the compact I am proposing to you is meant to do."

In September 2000, the Heads of State and Government adopted the United Nations Millennium Declaration (A/RES/55/2), which resolved to develop strong partnerships with the private sector and civil society organizations in pursuit of development and poverty eradication. In December of that same year, the UN General Assembly adopted a somewhat cautious resolution entitled "Towards Global Partnerships" (A/RES/55/215), which, citing the Millennium Declaration, called upon the UN Secretary-General to seek the views of member states on ways and means to improve co-operation between the UN and all relevant partners, in particular the private sector, and calls upon the Secretary General to seek the views of all relevant partners, in particular the private sector, on how to enhance their collaboration with the UN. A year later, in December 2001, the General Assembly adopted another resolution (A/RES/56/76) proclaiming stronger support for PPIs under the heading in which it:

> "invites the UN system to continue to adhere a common approach to partnerships which, without imposing undue rigidity in partnership agreements, includes the following principles: common purpose, transparency, bestowing no unfair advantage among any partner of the United Nations, mutual benefits and mutual respect, accountability, respect for the modalities of the United Nations, striving for balanced representation of relevant partners from developed and developing countries and countries with economies in transition, and not compromising the independence and neutrality of the United nations system in general and the agencies in particular." ....
> "Stresses further the need for the Member States to further discuss partnerships and to consider, in appropriate intergovernmental consultation, ways and means to enhance cooperation between the United nations and all relevant partners, inter alia, from the developing countries…"

Changes in similar directions also occurred within UN agencies, programmes and funds. The UN Funds and Programmes report to the General Assembly (GA) and the UN Economic and Social Council (A/RES/48/162), and therefore follow discussions and decisions that take place at the UN level. In her speech in April 1999 at the Harvard International Development Conference, the Executive Director of Unicef, Carol Bellamy, while acknowledging the statements of Kofi Annan, warned that:

"It would be dangerous to assume that the goals of the private sector are somehow synonymous with those of the United Nations, because emphatically they are not."

Bellamy also said that:

"… in coming together with the private sector, the UN must carefully, and constantly, appraise the relationship." (Bellamy 1999)

Since 1999, however, Unicef has proceeded in a less cautious manner. According to Bellamy (1999), in 1999, Unicef had the most extensive corporate involvement of any single UN agency. Recently, Unicef has been roundly criticised for launching alliances with, for example, fast food company McDonald's and soft drinks company Coca Cola, both known more for their marketing skills than for promoting healthy lifestyles.

When taking office in 1998 as Director-General of the WHO, Dr Gro Harlem Brundtland announced that:

"The private sector has an important role to play both in technology development and the provision of services. We need open and constructive relations with the private sector and the industry, knowing where our roles differ and where they may complement each other. I invite the industry to join in a dialogue on the key issues facing us. To this end I will propose the creation of a WHO-industry roundtable and convene a first meeting before the end of the year." (Brundtland 1998)

WHO, as the specialized UN organization on health, receives its mandate from its governing bodies, the World Health Assembly (WHA) and the executive board (EB). So far, the WHA has not given the WHO an explicit mandate to engage in close co-operation with the private sector. In January 2000, the EB received a report from the Director-General outlining a corporate strategy for the WHO secretariat (EB 105/3) and another on the topic of public-private partnerships for health (EB 105/8). A year later, in January 2001, the Executive Board received a report by the secretariat entitled 'Guidelines on working with the private sector to achieve health outcomes' with an annex on the draft guidelines. Althought the report was only given for the EB to note, the draft guidelines provoked harsh criticism in the EB meeting (EB107/SR/11 and EB197/SR/12), and the EB resolved to have an electronic discussion about the guidelines and their further elaboration. Despite the critique, shortly after this meeting, the Director-General endorsed the guidelines as managerial tools for the WHO Secretariat (EB 107/20), without the electronic discussion ever taking place. Instead the matter was discussed in November 2001 at an EB retreat, a gathering that does not publish minutes of what was discussed. In January 2002, the EB briefly discussed the Director-General's report on public-private interactions for health again and reiterated some, albeit toned down, concerns about the risks of interactions with the private sector. (EB109/SR/4)

As already mentioned, the UN Funds are guided by the decisions and policies of the UN General Assembly. Unicef's specific areas of action are guided by the 1990 World Summit for Children and its follow up in 2002, the UN's Special Session for Children. The document resulting from the 2002 Special Session entitled "A World Fit for Children" (A/S-27/19/Rev.1) acknowledges the role of the private sector in mobilising resources. It encourages corporate social responsibility and *inter alia* the enhancement of partnerships with business, while also stressing that corporations must abide by national legislation

Earlier in the 1990s, the outcome of another UN conference, the 1994 International Conference on Population and Development (ICPD) had mentioned partnerships. The ICPD's programme of action includes a chapter on partnerships with the non-governmental sector in which a sub-chapter is devoted to the profit-oriented sector (United Nations 1994). In 1995, an executive board decision at UNDP/UNFPA supported the broad outline of the future UNFPA programme, which has to be implemented in full accordance with the ICPD's Programme of Action (EB decision 95/15). The follow-up meeting for ICPD in 1999 also stressed the role of partnerships.

As can be seen from all these developments, the UN mandate to increase its interactions with the private sector had been strengthening during the 1990s – although *after* steps had already been taken in that direction. In the case of WHO, it is less clear whether there is an explicit mandate from the WHA for increased private sector involvement or not.

This change within the United Nations and its agencies did not just happen by itself, come out of nowhere or go uncontested. It has been strongly debated and largely is a result of constraints in the UN's funding, pressures from some member states and a strong commitment by the Secretary-General to take the UN in that direction.

3. Current collaboration with the corporate sector

3.1 Definitions of PPPs and PPIs

Regardless of the heated discussions and debates about PPPs, the UN does not have a common definition of what it means by PPPs. The term "partnership" is used very loosely to refer to almost any kind of relationship (Nelson 2002), including corporate sponsorship and policy dialogues. Drawing on a number of sources, Nelson uses the following definition: "Partnership is a voluntary and collaborative agreement between one or more partners of the UN system and non-state actors, in which all participants agree to work together to achieve a common purpose or undertake a specific task and to share risks, responsibilities, resources, competencies and benefits (Nelson 2002,

46). According to Tesner with Kell, a UN-business partnership is a mutually beneficial agreement between one or more UN bodies and one or more corporate partners to work towards common objectives based on the comparative advantage of each, with a clear understanding of respective responsibilities and the expectation of due credit for every contribution (Tesner with Kell 2000). There have been efforts under the auspices of the UN Fund for International Partnerships (UNFIP) to develop a common definition for partnerships. In their article looking at health-related partnerships, Buse and Walt define partnerships as a collaborative relationship which transcends national boundaries and brings together at least three parties, among them a corporation (and/ or industry association) and an intergovernmental organization, so as to achieve a shared health-creating goal on the basis of a mutually agreed division of labour (Buse and Walt 2000). Meanwhile, the WHO is increasingly using the term "interactions" for its collaboration with the corporate sector, while Unicef uses the terms "alliance" for a public-private partnership and "ally" to describe a corporate partner.

In this paper, the term PPI is used as a general term to refer to the various forms of interaction between the private sector and the UN. In general, PPP is used to refer to interactions that imply that the private sector is included in an agenda setting, policy-making and priority-setting exercise. But as PPPs are used so loosely in the original UN context, in being faithful to the original texts, some confusion over the terms is unavoidable. This paper uses the terms "business" and "corporations" to refer to those sectors which are clearly for-profit, while the term "private sector" is used to refer to the for-profit sector *and* to various non-profit entities. Many foundations, moreover, are closely linked with corporations. In interviews with UN officials, it became clear that while many could see that corporate money might involve some risks, they generally thought that money from foundations did not.

The various kinds of partnerships have been classified in a number of ways. There is no formal or commonly agreed categorization for different types of cooperation between the UN and business (Nelson 2002), and the typologies within even one organisation differs from one text to another. The typologies used in the guidelines of the UN, Unicef and WHO for interactions with the for-profit sector are described in the Annex. In principle, all list contributions in-cash and in-kind, advocacy and common efforts towards a particular goal.

3.2. The United Nations

The expectations of collaboration with the private sector are manifold. For the UN, official general expectations have included the promotion of stability, economic and political transition, increased levels of trade and economic development (Kofi Annan, 1997 SG/SM/6153). The expectations on the part of the UN, governments, business and civil society have also been summarised as:

1) business resource mobilization
2) greater support for UN values and activities;
3) increased innovation;
4) shared learning, increased trust and mutual understanding;
5) better understanding of boundaries and expectations; and
6) business benefits (Nelson 2002, 39).

In practice, many of the hopes of PPPs have centred on increased funding from corporations. The declining levels of OECD development assistance to the UN, which became particularly acute in the 1990s, made the private sector seem like a potentially important source of funding (Utting 2000). Lately, it has become evident that, at least in the GHPPPs, industry and industry associations have not generally come up with significant funding for PPPs. More recently, many have stated that the agencies are not looking just for funding from corporations, but also for knowledge and expertise. Furthermore, it has often been emphasised that the UN will have little relevance for global policy-making unless it engages in close collaboration with the private sector.

According to Unicef's executive director, Carol Bellamy (1999):

"One widely talked about rationale for the UN working in partnership with industry and the business community is based on the assumption that the resources of government are not plentiful enough – and that if development is to succeed, we must look for those resources in the private sector and in the marketplace.
I would submit that this is a very poor rational for partnership. It is poor for two reasons: first, it is based on the mistaken idea that governments should be allowed to shrink their responsibility and as the leading players in development ... Second, it is a poor rationale for partnership because it is based on a limited and almost patronising view that the private sector can bring to a relationship with the UN – namely, money."

According to Unicef's director of its Private Sector Division, Alejandro Palacios (interview in October 2002), the Unicef's expectations for private sector collaboration are: 1) funds, 2) direct programme support from corporations, 3) research and development capacity, and 4) influence over governments.

3.3 Global Compact

As already stated, the UN's Secretary-General, Kofi Annan announced the Global Compact at the World Economic Forum in 1999, when he challenged world business leaders to "embrace and enact" nine principles covering human rights, labour and environment. It has since become clear that the Compact has not intention of verifying whether the companies really have incorporated the nine principles into their core practices. According to an interview with a staff member at the Compact office in October 2002, the companies become part of the Compact once they have written to the Secretary-General and once they have submitted one example of their socially-responsible conduct linked to any of the nine principles. Apart from initial screening to check that the company is not manufacturing landmines or weapons, the Global Compact office does not screen them companies further. If a Global Compact company were to be accused of repeated misconduct, the office would initiate a dialogue with the company and eventually possibly exclude that company. So far, the Compact office has not felt the need for a dialogue with any of the companies that have subscribed to the Compact, because they believe that the breaches reported have been too general (interview in October 2002).

Many NGOs have been very critical of the Global Compact as a concept, as well as of the lack of vigilance over the practices of the companies that are part of it. They have also criticized the Global Compact for providing companies with an effective tool to enhance their positive image and influence, without really making any obligations as to their conduct. Critical NGO groups have expressed concern that the UN is lending its hand via the Global Compact and other "partnerships" with transnational companies to "bluewashing" corporate names through corporate association with the UN and its leaders. They have called for a corporate-free UN (*see* web sites of Corporate Europe Observateory, http://www.xs4all.nl/~ceo and CorpWatch, http://www.corpwatch.org/).

There is, indeed, considerable confusion about the role of the Global Compact even among UN offices and programmes. For example, one UNFIP staff member thought that a company that is part of the Compact had been closely vetted as a suitable candidate for partnership with UN agencies, and she planned to start actively encouraging companies within the Global Compact to build PPPs with UN agencies.

3.4 WHO

A changed policy environment in which increased attention is paid to the private sector globally, nationally and locally, as well as less clear demarcations between the private and the public sector, prompted WHO to elaborate its thinking on public-private partnerships in the late 1990s. As part of the renewal process of WHO's "Health for All" policy, a working group on partnerships for health was formed (Kickbush and Quick 1998). It was, however, only after Gro Harlem Brundtland was nominated by the executive board to be elected for Director General of WHO in January 1998, particularly after she took office in July 1998, that partnerships and other interactions with the corporate sector started to be promoted within WHO as important shifts in organisational policy. In addition to alliances, there are today more than 60 WHO ongoing partnerships with the corporate sector, and the organisation has received a significant increase in corporate funding (*see* Box 1).

Box 1. Corporate funding at WHO

WHO's budget is made up from "assessed contributions" from Member States (the regular budget) and from voluntary contributions from a variety of resources (the extrabudgetary resources). The assessed contributions from member states have declined in real terms by about 20% over the past ten years, while the extrabudgetary resources have increased. The regular budget now comprises only 41% of the total budget (Motchane 2002), but was still more than half the budget at the beginning of the 1990s (Vaughan et al. 1995).

As can be seen from the table below, the increase in total extrabudgetary resources between the two biannual budgets of 1998–1999 and 2000–2001 was 65%. Governments still remain the major providers of extrabudgetary funds, but the rise of private sector funding including from corporations and NGOs [1], has risen sharply, and now accounts for more than 10% of WHO's total budget, or almost 20% of the total voluntary contributions. While it is certainly welcome that governments attempt to compensate for the declining regular budget, this increase in extrabudgetary funds can make WHO more vulnerable to undue influence, because it needs to continue receiving high levels of funding to keep up its ongoing work. This undue influence does not apply only to the corporate sector, but to all sources of voluntary contributions which are pledged on annual or biannual bases. But the increase in corporate funding is certainly the most problematic in terms of preserving the integrity of the Organization.

Table: **Extrabudgetary contributions per biennium and change in contributions from one biennium to another (unpublished data from WHO)**

	1998–2001 (US$)	2000–2001(US$)	Change (%)
Total voluntary contributions	742,361,526	1,221,728,350	65
Source of extrabudgetary funding	1998–1999 (% of total EBF)	2000–2001 (% of total EBF)	Change from 98–99 to 00–01 in US$ (% of increase)
Member States	60	70	62
UN & Intergovernmental Organizations	8	5	4
Foundations	17	14	37
Private sector & NGOs	13	17	119
Local Governments and City Authorities	2	2	18

[1] The NGO funding includes, for example the corporate funding for WHO, directed through the US Unicef Association for tax purposes

In January 2000, the Director General of the WHO launched a Commission on Macroeconomics and Health (CMH). The 15-member CMH, led by economist Jeffrey Sachs of Harvard University, included health economists from various international organizations. Its broad brief was to look at the effects of health on economic growth. The Commission's Report was delivered nearly two years later in December 2001. It recommended, among other things, a substantial increase in health sector resources in low- and middle-income countries. The CMH Report stressed the role that public-private partnerships could play and cautioned the governing bodies of WHO not to constrain WHO's work by raising concerns about conflicts of interest (Commission on macroeconomics and health, 2001).

For the future, the Director-General of WHO has given the following priorities on WHO's work on public-private interactions for health:

1) support to member states on public-private interactions;
2) commodity donation programmes;
3) lower prices for commodities;
4) product research and development;
5) advocacy and behavioural change; and
6) corporate workplace health programmes.

The Director General also pointed to the need for staff training on issues related to private-sector involvement and conflict of interest (WHO EB109/4).

3.4 Unicef and UNFPA

The UN Funds are reliant on voluntary contributions. Unicef has always had significant collaboration with non-state actors. Non-state resources have traditionally comprised about one-third of its total income, mostly from selling Christmas cards and other products, as well as from individual contributions through its National Committees (UNICEF 1995). The goodwill and admiration for Unicef's mission has been evident in the way in which citizens have given their time for Unicef's work by collecting money for Unicef, unlike any other UN agency. But in recent years, Unicef has increasingly emphasised the importance of the corporate sector. Currently, about 6–8% of Unicef's total funding originates from corporate sources, but the proportion of corporate funding is expected to rise to 10% by the year 2005.

In an interview with the Unicef staff responsible for Unicef's private sector collaboration, it became clear that some of Unicef's expectations are very far reaching. For example, it was hoped that collaboration with the Coca-Cola company could eventually help in solving distribution problems of HIV/AIDS drugs and that the involvement of Finnish mobile phone company Nokia in the Global Movement for Children could be helpful in convincing the Finnish government to increase its funding for Unicef. According to Buse and Walt, in practice, many of Unicef's partnerships are limited to fund-raising and image enhancement (Buse and Walt 2000).

One of UNFPA's traditional roles have been to procure contraceptives. UNFPA's major PPP, the UNFPA Private-Sector Initiative is helping to match contraceptive producers with national level contraceptive needs. Under this initiative, pharmaceutical companies have agreed to set reasonable prices while governments have agreed to lower the trade barriers for the companies to enter the country and to conduct market research (UNFPA 1999). The search for more substantial private financing for UNFPA is only now being initiated.

3.5 Major Global Health-Related Public-Private Partnerships (GHPPPs)

The new Millennium has seen the emergence of a new form of major GHPPPs that aim to deal with essential public health issues by creating new structures largely outside the auspices of the United Nations. The first to emerge in 1999 was the Global Alliance for Vaccination and Immunization (GAVI), which has since been used as a model for constructing other new partnerships, such as the Global Fund to Fight Against AIDS, Tuberculosis and Malaria (GFATM) and the Global Alliance for Improved Nutrition (GAIN) focusing on supplying micronutrients. GAIN is still being put together after it was announced at the 20002 UN Special Session on Children, but has already attracted extensive criticism both in terms of its substance and in terms of the business partners involved (Zimmerman 2002)[2].

---

[2] Many NGOs have critisized the approach on their web sites, see for example Commercial Alert web site, www.commercialalert.org, for reporters, Aug 26, 2002

Figure 1   Organogram of GAVI and the Vaccine fund
(Based on a figure provided by GAVI secretariat)

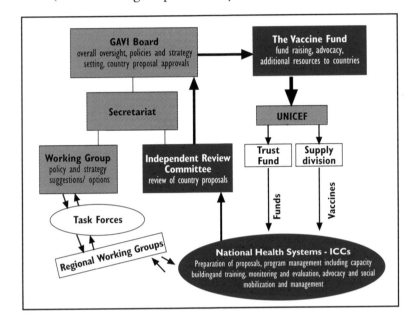

GAVI Board members include renewable members from WHO, UNICEF, the World Bank and the Bill and Melinda Gates Foundation and rotating members from OECD countries (3) and developing countries (2), industry (1 from OECD, other from a developing country), 1 foundation (currently UN Foundation), 1 NGO (currently Sierra Leone Cross Society), 1 research institute (currently Institute Pasteur) and 1 technical health institute (currently US Center for Disease Control). The balance is therefore on OECD country representation. The GAVI secretariat is housed in the premises of Unicef in Geneva.

The GAVI Working Group facilitates the implementation of the decisions and policies of the GAVI Board. It holds meeting four times a year, as well as weekly teleconferences. The Working group includes 3 representatives from intergovernmental agencies (the World Bank, Unicef, WHO), 3 from GAVI, the Vaccines Fund and the Children's Vaccine Programme of PATH; 1 industry representative, 1 US university; 1 representative from a developing country Ministry of Health and 1 from the USAID .

The review committee has nine members, six of whom are from developing countries, two from countries of the former Soviet Union or Eastern Europe, and one from the US.

The National Interagency Coordinating Committee (ICC) at national levels include representation from ministries and partner agencies such as WHO, Unicef, the World Bank, European Community, bilateral donors – as well as private sector.

The Vaccine Fund makes funding decisions on projects and programmes based on GAVI Board's recommendations. The Trust Fund housed at Unicef reports to the Vaccine Fund. The Vaccine Fund reports to the biggest funder, the Bill & Melinda Gates Foundation.

The organizational structure of GAVI (*see* Figure 1) is fairly complicated, which makes it difficult to trace the lines of accountability. For example, the Vaccine Fund is the financial instrument of GAVI, but reports to the Bill and Melinda Gates Foundation. The role of the UN agencies vary in these partnerships. While GAVI still has WHO and Unicef as voting members on its board, GFATM includes them only as non-voting members. Within GAIN, only one international organization (UN organization or other multilateral) will have a seat. In relation to GFATM, some partners have articulated an intention to take distance from the UN system (Phillips 2002). Nevertheless, GAVI, GFATM and GAIN have insisted that their staff will have UN privileges, such as tax exemptions and diplomatic status. Therefore, these partnerships are technically housed in UN agencies but are independent bodies. The role of the governing bodies of the UN agencies in these partnership structures in which decision-making is shared between a variety of partners is complicated. All these three GHPPPs deal with essential public health issues for which policy-making and agenda setting should be at the core of UN health-related agencies.

The most striking feature of the governance structure is that the GHPPPs include the industry in policy-making and agenda setting. Although they all have industry representation in their decision-making bodies, they lack mechanisms to deal with conflicts of interests. GAVI has a conflict-of-interest policy for the technical review panel experts, but none for the other bodies. A GFATM representative said in an interview that there were no conflicts of interest since everyone on the various governing structures acted in their personal capacity, not on behalf of the constituency they represented. The GFATM secretariat interviewee saw no problem with a representative of the pharmaceutical research and development industry sitting in a working group which was drafting GFATM's policy to procure pharmaceutical drugs, even though there have been heated debates over whether generic pharmaceuticals should be included in the procurement policy or not.

Box 2. Global Alliance for Vaccination and Immunization (GAVI)

Global efforts to immunize the world's children have been remarkably successful. From less than 5% coverage of the world's children against six major killer diseases (diphtheria, tetanus, whooping cough, polio, measles and tuberculosis) in the mid-1970s, coverage had reached the Unicef's target of 80% by 1990. In 1974 WHO had launched an Expanded Programme on Immunisation (EPI). The EPI was accelerated with the Universal Childhood Immunisation (UCI) campaign. Having reached the target, however, the effort began to break apart, because of a number of reasons, such as war, new diseases, donor fatigue and a change of leadership at WHO, although there were plans to not only sustain coverage, but also to reach 90% coverage. In the 1990s, immunisation coverage deteriorated in most of the world's poorest countries. By 2000, global coverage had dropped to 75%. In 19 countries, diphtheria, tetanus and polio coverage dropped to below 50%. In Nigeria, overall coverage dropped in less than a decade from 80% in 1990 to 27% in 1998. (Hardon 2001) The deterioration of the vaccines programmes was also seen in the decline in demand for basic vaccines from Unicef in the later half of the 1990s (Jarrett 2002). In 2000, GAVI was launched at the World Economic Forum with an initial donation of US$750 million from the Bill and Melinda Gates Foundation.

Aims

The aim of GAVI is to save children's lives and people's health through the widespread use of vaccines. The founding members included WHO, UNICEF, the World Bank, the Bill and Melinda Gates Children's Vaccines Program, the Rockefeller Foundation, the International Federation of Pharmaceutical Manufacturers' Association and some national governments.

Funding

In January 2002, the total funds received for GAVI activities were US$1,089 million. So far, in addition to the initial US$750 million, only an additional US$339 million had been committed, all from governmental bilateral sources. No additional corporate money had been forthcoming. The Gates Foundation money is committed over five years. Funds beyond the initial five years have not yet been secured.

The performance of GAVI

Within a year after its launch, some new funds had already reached countries. But only US$ 90 million of a total US$ 375 million available was disbursed over the first couple of years.

Concerns (Hardon 2000, Starling et al. 2001) :

- The priorities in terms of vaccines have been distorted. Some 75% of the funding approved for the first two years have been for the use of new vaccines, mainly against Hepatitis B.
- The priorities in terms of countries receiving assistance has been: of the 23 countries selected for support, only 9 have an immunisation coverage of less than 75%. Furthermore, the countries with the lowest coverages have received the lowest funds.
- Priorities in terms of in-country equity are biased: children who have not been vaccinated within a basic programme are likely to remain unvaccinated, while those who have been given basic vaccines will receive the additional new vaccines.
- The initiative is not sustainable as yet. Funds for GAVI are guaranteed for five years only and alternative funding mechanisms have not been developed. The costs of vaccine programmes using newly-introduced vaccines have increased substantially compared to the costs of the routine EPI.

The core of GAVI's business (Box 2) has, in practice, been to introduce new vaccines to countries that have not used them so far. The core business of GFATM (Box 3), meanwhile, will in practice be to introduce HIV/AIDS drugs, both for preventing and for treating the disease. It has been calculated that more than 60% of GFATM's first grants were for pharmaceuticals. GAIN will focus on fortifying food. Overall, all three have a narrow, technology focus that can accommodate industry interests. GAVI, for instance, has been shown to focus on expensive new vaccines (Hardon 2000). GFATM has reportedly been under strong pressure to concentrate on procuring patent-protected pharmaceuticals. But the GFATM board decided in its October meeting that they would not exclude generic pharmaceuticals (McNeil 2002). With management consultant McKinsey & Company on GFATM'S board, one should look critically at the way in which GFATM might affect the service delivery systems in countries, because of its focus on the private sector.

Box 3. Global Fund to Fight AIDS, Tuberculosis and Malaria (GFATM)

The Global Fund to Fight AIDS, Tuberculosis and Malaria (GFATM) is a combination of several initiatives, including the three diseases approach announced at the G8 meeting in July 2000 in Okinawa aimed at fighting AIDS, malaria and tuberculosis, and the access to treatment campaign led by a group of NGOs fighting for access to HIV/AIDS treatments.

Aims

As the name of the Fund indicates, it focuses on the three diseases of HIV/AIDS, tuberculosis and malaria. It is clear, however, that the bulk of the funds will go towards HIV/AIDS. Much of the Fund's focus has been on pharmaceuticals to prevent and treat these diseases.

Structure

GFATM is a funding instrument, not an implementing organisation. GFATM has taken GAVI as a model for its governance structures. GFATM has an independent secretariat housed by WHO in Geneva. Its voting board consists of representatives of seven donor governments, seven developing-country governments, two NGOs, one foundation and one from the corporate sector. Non-voting members include a WHO, a UNAIDS and a NGO representative of the community of people living with HIV/AIDS, TB or malaria, and a Swiss member. The World Bank manages the money as a trustee. A 17-member technical review panel, consisting mainly of experts in the three diseases, review the proposals. There is also an informal partners forum gathering every two years.

Funding

GFATM aims to raise US$ 7-10 billion in funds. So far, it has gathered pledges for US$2.1 billion. Although this is substantially less than sought for, it is impressive for an initiative in its early stages. Of the US$ 2.1 billion pledged so far, 2 billion has come from public sources (bilateral and European Community), and just US$ 100 million from the private sources, (Bill and Melinda Gates Foundation). During the last half year, only US$ 200 million has been pledged for GFATM. In terms of GFATM's sustainability, it is of concern that a substantial amount of the total funds available have already been allocated to recipients and little new money is now coming in. It is furthermore concerning that much of the policies and mechanisms are still being developed, while grants have already been announced.

Concerns

- Democratic accountability is less clear than in UN-hosted programmes. The role of UNAIDS and WHO, the UN organisations on whose mandate the three diseases primarily fall, are relegated to non-voting board members. Industry is represented in policy-making and agenda setting positions.
- No substantial new funding for development aid has been forthcoming. About 95% of the pledged funds are from public resources, mostly taken away from other development aid.
- Funds are directed towards three selected diseases, which may compromise the possibilities for the development of more comprehensive health systems.
- GFATM is a funding body. The necessary technical assistance at country level should be ensured at all stages of the programme.
- Proper policies and mechanisms still not in place.
- There is concern that too much emphasis will be placed on funding purchases of medical products.
- GFATM with its resources, policies and implementation mechanisms may have a big impact on existing health systems, particularly on primary health care structures and capacities. This should be carefully monitored.
- The focus on clear and measurable results may limit activities to selected interventions and give less emphasis to initiatives with intersectoral working methods and long-term goals.

Pressures on these global health-related public-private partnerships to show progress and efficiency have compromised the development of these entities. In the case of GAVI, there are reports of governments being unreasonable prompted to make decisions at a country level, which they are then unable to implement, partly because they cannot act with the speed GAVI insists upon and partly for reasons relating more to GAVI itself or to vaccine availability (Starling et al. 2001; Brugha and Walt, 2001). In the case of GFATM, this striving for apparent efficiency resulted in the fund giving unreasonable timetables to countries to prepare and submit their proposals for the first round of grants, even though GFATM could then not act on its funding decisions because of its own lack of policies, mechanisms and systems at the time.

While these new structures have been justified on the grounds of gains in efficiency, such efficiency is compromised by the enormous use of staff time from the UN secretariat and governmental development agencies to construct the initiatives and their procedures, as well as to give backing in substance areas, and to deal with much of the administrative issues. Many services of the Funds are being contracted out. In the case of GFATM, concerns have been raised over the top heavy structure of the Fund. Efficiency, in terms of Fund staff time per dollar dispersed, may still be relatively high because of the size of the grants given, but in this respect there are still concerns related to the efficient use of money and the absorption capacity of that money at national levels.

The GHPPPs have introduced new business-like thinking. GAVI has been praised for introducing results-based funding systems in the health area. In practice, results-based thinking has not proved effective so far. It has introduced increased demands for parallel monitoring and reporting systems, although there have been efforts to integrate these within existing systems.

4. Procedures at the health-related UN agencies for selecting and approving partnerships

The UN agencies have insufficient procedures in place for managing their private sector interactions (Mezzalama and Ouedraogo 1999, Buse and Waxman 2001). In recent years, many of them have been developing guidelines and procedures to fill this gap.

Guidelines issued in July 2000 by the Secretary General are intended to serve as a common framework for all UN organizations (that is, the UN secretariat, and UN funds and programmes). These guidelines encouraged the individual organizations to develop more specific guidelines of their own in accordance with their particular mandates and activities. The WHO guidelines were endorsed by the WHO Director-General in 2001. The draft version was widely circulated for consultation, but despite the criticism it received from WHO's Executive Board (and some heavy-weight NGOs), the guidelines were endorsed without change by the Director-General as a managerial tool for WHO's Secretariat. Meanwhile, preparation of the Unicef Guidelines and Manual for Working with the Business Community started in 1998 and the Guidelines were issued in 2001. While the UN guidelines and WHO guidelines are readily available, the Unicef guidelines are not. Only a two-page summary of the Unicef guidelines is available for anyone outside Unicef. The following information about the Unicef guidelines is based both on this summary and on various interviews with Unicef staff, as well as with the Finnish Unicef Association. UNFPA drafted its guidelines in 2000, but they have not been endorsed because of change in the organisation's upper management. It has recently finalized its guidelines, but has not yet made them available because it first wants to test them in the field. The UNFPA guidelines are mainly based on the policies and guidelines of UNDP and the World Bank. The major features of the UN, WHO and Unicef guidelines are presented in the Annex 1.

Two distinct processes for decision-making on private sector interactions should be involved. The first involves analysing the actual content or substance of the interaction and searching for the best form of interaction with the best partners. The second involves looking at the characteristics of the private sector entities that are potential partners in an interaction and then choosing the private sector partner. It has been said that in practice, however, it is more often the private sector entity that is active in seeking a UN partner rather than a UN agency. Thus, in many cases, the process involves only assessing a proposed activity and screening a potential partner which have both already presented themselves. Feeling pressure to engage in PPPs, some civil servants seem to think that engaging in a PPP is in itself advantageous. "Since the PPPs are by definition mutually beneficial, it is assumed that they are", said one UN official.

Within WHO, the relevant cluster assesses the substance of the partnership. In principle, the Legal Office and the Department of Government and Private Sector Relations deal with all WHO's potential private sector interactions, but in practice all initiatives do not pass through these structures. Many clusters have ongoing partnerships that have not gone through the process. Moreover, several major initiatives, such as GAIN, were decided upon in WHO's upper echelons without being recommended either on substance grounds or after partner screening and with the structure involving difficult conflict-of-interest dilemmas. How WHO will take part in GAIN, however, was in June 2002 not clear to anyone interviewed.

In Unicef, its Private Sector Division is the organization's focal point for PPIs. Any international PPI is meant to be approved by this Division. A Co-ordination Committee reviews all PPI proposals about which there are some doubts and all interactions that involve the use of Unicef's name, logo or emblem. Unicef's office in Geneva is charged with corporate screening. While Unicef claims that it rigorously screens its partners, it has recently launched several initiatives that violate its own criteria. Fast food company McDonald's, for instance, has been found guilty in court of abusing children through their advertising and of using child labour (Vidal 1997, see also http://www.mcspotlight.org/case/ for the McDonalds court trial). GAIN's initial partners, meanwhile, included a tobacco affiliate and company accused of infringing the baby milk Code, neither one of which should have passed Unicef screening. As the GAIN initiative has progressed, these two companies are no longer mentioned as being part of the initiative. UNFPA, as already mentioned, had not, as of October 2001, made a decision on the organisational structure to manage the selection of its private sector partners.

In some agencies, the possibility that PPIs or PPPs may involve risks is clearly not widely acknowledged. Several officials interviewed were caught by surprise when asked about the possible risks. In an interview with UNFPA, it was apparent that staff had not thought to include potential risks in its planning for devising national training agendas, although its guidelines do supposedly include information on risks and conflicts of interest. The UNAIDS interviewee said that it was generally thought that any PPI would be beneficial if it served to diminish the stigma of HIV/AIDS. As of June 2002, UNAIDS had engaged in practically any partnership that had been suggested to it, although it was starting to review that policy.

There is an ongoing plan within the UN system to devise a common corporate selection tool, in which five UN agencies, funds and programmes, including WHO and UNFPA, plan to participate. The common assessment will be drawn up as a reduced version of the Global Compact. It is still not clear whether this common screening would lead to all organizations assessing their partners on the same grounds, or whether individual organisations would include some criteria of their own that would reflect their particular concerns stemming from their respective mandates. In this common endeavour, a private firm dealing in sustainable investments, Calward, will be contracted to perform these assessments. Unicef is not taking part in this process, because it has its own screening system in its Geneva office.

5. PPPs in global health-policy making

As indicated in this paper, interactions between the UN and the private sector have changed considerably during the last decade both in their volume and in their nature. While the UN certainly needs to interact with the private sector several ways, these interactions become problematic when extended to "partnerships" in which corporations – or corporate philanthropists – have a say in defining public policy priorities and setting agendas. The manner of the interaction between the UN and the private sector should be tailored to fit the particular aim of each issue to be tackled. For issues that benefit from corporate interactions, possible avenues include policy dialogues, contracting services and corporate sponsorship. In addition to the risks and problems outlined above, forming a partnership implies considerable transaction costs, which should not be overlooked when the advantages of a partnership are considered.

All organisations emphasise that PPIs and PPPs are not only about fund-raising, but corporate sponsorship, in-cash or in-kind, is still the predominant content of interactions. Private sector interactions have, however, increasingly started to involve corporations in policy-making, agenda setting and priority setting.

The success of the GHPPPs in drawing funds that would not otherwise have been used for development aid has not been impressive so far. While funding from the Bill and Melinda Gates Foundation has been essential for GAVI, GFATM has not received any significant funding from outside the public sector. More particularly, they have *all* been unsuccessful in attracting funds from industry. This raises concerns about the funding base of the more traditional avenues for supplying development aid for health, that existing development aid will increasingly be channelled through GHPPPs.

In the analysis that follows, the emphases is on some observed or potential problems, concerns that have been raised, and necessary safeguards to avoid them. Most of the problems and concerns are not linked solely to specific public-private interactions, but to a broader shift in the policy paradigm, which in itself has been pushed and supported by some member states. Many of the problems and concerns are, however, amplified by the increased corporate collaboration.

5.1. The policy paradigm

Global policy-making is affected by increased globalisation and market orientation. Serious efforts need to be taken to ensure that this shift in the policy paradigm does not affect the fundamental aims of UN organizations, such as those outlined in the Preamble of the UN Charter (cited at the beginning of this paper). If policy-making on essential public health matters is removed from the auspices of the UN system, there is a risk that the relevance of the UN for global public health will diminish. Indeed, there is some evidence to suggest that one aim of some proponents of GHPPPs has been precisely that: to undermine the role of the UN system in policy-making (*see*, for example Phillips 2002). Moreover it has been argued that establishing independent partnerships with shared responsibilities, such as GAVI and GFATM, would help to circumvent the governing bodies of WHO (Yamey 2002).

According to Utting, a significant shift in UN policy towards transnational corporations (TNCs) occurred in the 1980s, partly reflecting the influence of neo-liberalism, such that by the early 1990s, various regulatory initiatives ground to halt. Meanwhile, voluntary codes of conduct have had a limited impact on the conduct of corporations as a whole (Utting 2000, Richter 2000a, Jenkins 2001). This shift from regulation to voluntary codes and corporate social responsibility is also reflected in Kofi Annan's statement to the 1999 World Economic Forum (quoted above) in which he called for voluntary measures to influence corporate conduct instead of regulation. While social responsibility of corporations is certainly welcome, it is important to notice that efforts towards obligatory regulations may be indirectly – and at times even directly – undermined by emphases on voluntary codes, corporate social responsibility and PPPs (Richter 2000a, Utting 2000).

As corporations gain more power in global public-policy-making through PPPs, it becomes more difficult to ensure that public interests remain at the core of such decisions. It is obvious that increased collaborations with the corporate sector which have emerged with PPPs not only reflect a shift in the policy paradigm, but also reinforce such a shift and may undermine regulatory and normative efforts. For example, the partnership of the five UN agencies with five transnational pharmaceutical companies to supply pharmaceutical drugs at reduced prices (even though only one of the five companies, Glaxo Wellcome, had disclosed its AIDS medicine discounts in eight months since the agreement) should be considered in the context of the concomitant struggle of certain developing countries and activist groups to test the flexibilities of the WTO's TRIPs Agreement (particularly on compulsory licensing and parallel imports, which are not actually mentioned in TRIPs) in order to help HIV-infected people in those countries (Gellman 2000, Freedman and Stecklow 2000, for more information on the TRIPS Agreement see the chapter by Koivusalo). Neglecting to give proper consideration to a clear conflict-of-interest was also apparent when the Commission of Macroeconomics and Health commissioned a background paper on the role of generic pharmaceuticals from the pharmaceutical research and development industry (Boseley 2002).

The very definition of a public-private partnership (Nelson 2002, 64), which implies a common agenda and priority setting together with the corporate sector, may impede UN agencies from acting in the public interest, because the UN agencies now have to accommodate private interests in their agendas and priorities as well. A major issue concerning the new major GHPPPs that are largely shifted outside the UN is a corporate sector with vested interests being involved in public-policy-making. This design reflects a fundamental neglect of acknowledging and dealing with conflicts of interest. In GAVI and GFATM, the industry representatives are involved in public-policy-making, even though industry has not provided any significant monetary resources. They are obviously assumed to provide the PPP with their knowledge and expertise. The corporate representatives are supposed to sit in their personal capacity and therefore conflicts of interest are said not to apply, because they deliver simply their expertise and advice. At the same time, however, the UN agencies are increasingly entrusted with administrative responsibilities for the GHPPPs, even though they have little official policy-making power. In this way, the GHPPPs have turned the traditional arrangement upside down: the corporate sector is entrusted with public-policy making and making decisions on the use of public money, while the UN is increasingly taking care of administrative practical matters and providing technical assistance – and even at times financial support.

5.2 Normative functions

The WHO has the norm and standard setting function in health, while Unicef, UNFPA and UNAIDS officially do not. For normative functions, therefore, the WHO in particular needs to safeguard its impartiality very carefully, but so do UN programmes and funds, such as Unicef, UNFPA and UNAIDS, as they carry UN prestige and through that some, albeit more informal, normative capacity.

Normative international organisations need to retain some technical functions at country level themselves, not only so as to have a real feel for realities at the country level, but also because implementation of norms and standards at the country level often require technical assistance and other resources. It is important that UN organisations with normative functions remain strong in their role, and do not turn themselves into development agencies placing undue emphases on implementing projects and programmes. The increasing amount of resources earmarked to development aid projects may distort the role of the normative organisation towards becoming a development agency.

As a result of several court cases against the tobacco industry in the United States, a large volume of internal documents from the tobacco industry became public. These documents revealed the tobacco industry's systematic efforts to undermine not only any progress on tobacco control, but also WHO as an organisation (Zeltner et al. 2000). This involved efforts to divert attention from the public health issues, to reduce budgets for the scientific and policy activities carried out by WHO, to pit other UN agencies against WHO and to convince developing countries that WHO's tobacco control was a "First World" agenda carried out at the expense of the developing countries. In their campaign against WHO tobacco companies hid behind a variety of organizations and international and scientific experts with hidden funding from the tobacco industry. As a result of WHO's total condemnation of tobacco, the strategies of the tobacco industry are likely to be more blunt than those of other industries with which WHO collaborates more closely. Nonetheless, the documents shed light on the various ways in which WHO can be infiltrated and undermined by industry.

For WHO, its most likely corporate ally is the pharmaceutical industry. It is, however, the very industry that has the most business interests at stake and the one, therefore, from which WHO should keep an adequate distance. In the late 1990s, concerns began to be raised that the distance was getting smaller and smaller. In 1999, when WHO issues its guidelines on hypertension, concerns were raised that industry had influenced the guidelines, resulting in recommendations that would lead to an overuse of pharmaceuticals to treat hypertension (Kopp, 2000). In 1999, WHO accepted a secondment from the pharmaceutical industry, Merck, Sharp and Dohme (MSD) to work in its tobacco programme. Many felt that accepting a secondment was unacceptable per se. In this particular case, concerns were raised that WHO's recommendations for the substances someone could take to help quit smoking were manufactured by a pharmaceutical company – the very same pharmaceutical company which had seconded its staff (*see*, for example, Hayes 2001, Utting 2000). In 2000, WHO was accused of stifling debate on infant feeding (Ferriman 2000, Richter, 2000b, Sokol, 2000). What is important here are both the observed shifts in WHO's normative advice and its perceived loss of integrity and the damage this entails.

At a country level, governments and especially their regulatory agencies need to be allowed to keep their impartiality to ensure that they maintain their proper normative capacities. The three major GHPPPs all require the public party to set up a co-ordination body with private partners at the country level. This body prepares the proposal to the particular partnership to request funding and co-ordinates the activities. Advocates of GHPPPs claim that this structure ensures coherent action at the country level. At the same time, however, it interferes with national policy-making patterns. Some features of the suggested partnership model risk impeding national regulatory functions, such as making demands on regulators to take part in the partnership or to give supportive statements on regulatory matters in anticipation of being granted resources. For example, under the heading "institutional requirements", GAIN suggests that the National Fortification Alliances from which GAIN accepts proposals, should include those public institutions mandated to organize nutritional surveillance, provide regulatory control of food quality and safety and implement pertinent policy and tax reforms. Such institutions should participate in the Alliance and express their commitment to it. Proposals to GAIN from a National Fortification Alliance should demonstrate a supportive government policy environment on matters of regulation, taxes and tariffs on food fortification – or plans to modify such policies as needed[3]. The UNFPA initiative for contraceptive supply required governments to remove any "unnecessary barriers" from the drug regulation (UNFPA 1999). Such proposals may make it mandatory for the government to remove perceived trade barriers, even in cases in which they are deemed to be in the interest of the population of the "recipient" country.

---

[3] For more information see the web site of GAIN (http://www.gainhealth.org/), from under Grants Programme, and RFP guidelines.

5.3 Policy coherence and broader policy aims

Assessments and evaluations of PPPs tend to be focused on the effects of a single PPP, often of a particular task of a programme or project. The wider framework tends to get less attention, except perhaps the aim of increased private sector involvement per se. It is outside the scope of this paper to analyse the pros and cons of PPPs for the corporate sector, but broader public-policy aims should be at the core of analysing PPPs from the perspective of public interests.

Partnerships rarely synchronise their activities with emerging processes within countries aimed at developing their national health systems (Yamey 2002). Neither do they typically link with other international processes, such as sector-wide approaches, poverty reduction strategies or programmes of debt relief for heavily indebted countries (Yamey 2002, Verheul and Rowson 2001, Starling et al. 2001).

This lack of policy coherence and perspective on broader policy aims is illustrated with three examples:

1) In the light of increasing health problems resulting from obesity and unhealthy diets, not only in the industrialized countries but also in developing countries, Unicef's recent launch of partnerships with McDonald's and Coca Cola has raised serious concerns (*See,* Ruskin 2002, Essential Information 2002). Besides the obvious damage to Unicef's image, the organisation is lending its (for now) positive image to these organizations and their marketing efforts, an image transfer that harms general nutritional policies with the unhealthy nutritional messages embedded in this partnership. According to Unicef's executive director, Carol Bellamy (Bellamy 2002) Unicef has not yet established a position on the complex nature of neither the obesity problem nor the best way to address it. It would, nonetheless, always be a good beginning to start with a "do no harm" policy and at least to make it clear that these partnerships do not aim to promote unhealthy eating habits.

2) In her speech at the 2001 World Economic Forum, Gro Harlem Brundtland (2001) said: "We need to protect patent rights. We need them to ensure the R&D will yield badly needed new tools and technologies. We need mechanisms to prevent re-export of lower priced drugs into richer economies. We must also recognize the concern of companies that lower prices in the developing world not be used as a lever to influence negotiations in countries that can easily afford to pay more." This statement is possibly understandable as a compromise in negotiations with the pharmaceutical industry on patented HIV/AIDS drugs. One wonders, however, whether a Director of the UN specialized agency for health should speak out in defence of property rights

and the protection of the high prices of the industry sector which has one of the largest profit margins in the world (Pear and Oppel 2002) when strengthened patent protection is acknowledged by many to be a major cause of the cost containment crises in health care services in most parts of the world, including in the North. There is little evidence that any increase in the industry's profit leads the industry to invest more in research and development on the diseases of the poor.

3) Funding from foundations is often perceived as unproblematic compared with funding from corporations. But there is a fine line between corporations and corporate foundations. According to Utting (2002), some might see the consolidation of the Bill and Melinda Gates Foundation at a time when Microsoft was being charged in the US with breaking anti-trust laws as more than coincidental. If it was in the public interest to strengthen anti-trust laws or to weaken patents, should the UN agencies take this into account when considering their policies on partnerships with this foundation or those like it?

5.4 Policy priorities

Certain private sector interactions may help to strengthen efforts towards a clearly defined task, since they often involve a concerted effort for a limited period of time for a limited goal. Private sector interactions, for instance, may be a practical arrangement to look for a technological solution to a defined problem.

Indeed, PPPs are more conducive to short-term technocratic solutions within a simplified results-based framework emphasizing narrow vertical interventions with pre-set indicators. While this may strengthen efforts towards a productive goal, it can also easily result in fragmented policies designed in the North, rather than more comprehensive long-term development polices in which the receiver remains in the driving seat. These approaches are conducive for vertical and medical intervention models and for fragmented organisation structures. Yamey (2002) has noted that:

"there is a tension between a donor-driven global partnership aiming for short term, high profile goals and the need for countries to broadly develop their health systems. Partnerships tend to 'pick the low hanging fruit' – they concentrate their efforts on getting quick results rather than building up the wider systems needed to address the broader burden of disease." (Yamey 2002)

Increased reliance on PPPs, and on narrow, earmarked funding more generally, may weaken efforts in areas where there are no obvious technological solutions, for instance, less attention paid to promoting breast-feeding but more to micronutrients within Unicef's policies.

Attempts to bring about increased accountability within PPPs have often included an increased orientation towards results-based approaches and monitoring requirements. In addition to corporations and foundations, also governmental donors can be more willing to give money for clearly-defined projects with concrete objectives and objects.

Corporations tend to give earmarked funding only and to have more of an interest in solutions that can be sold, that is, those which involve technologies, and they lean towards more expensive technologies. In worst cases, PPPs are closer to industrial policies than development policies. This problematic has perhaps most clearly illustrated in relation to the initiative to promote access to quality HIV medicines (Gellman 2000) and to the vaccine initiative, GAVI (Muraskin 2002). The introduction of expensive technological solutions diminishes not only the developmental and medical value of the financial contribution of these endeavours: it also diminishes the long-term sustainability of the effort itself. For example: GAVI has been criticized for introducing more expensive vaccines, sometimes without epidemiological evidence for their need (Hardon 2000, Starling et al. 2001, Brugha and Walt 2001). In the context of GFATM, there have been heated discussions about prevention versus cure, the role of pharmaceuticals in the prevention policies, and the possibility of including generics pharmaceuticals in addition to the more expensive brand name drugs. In its first round of grant giving, about 60% of GFATM's grant funding went on pharmaceutical purchases. GFATM has recently decided that generic drugs can be included under proper circumstances.

5.5 Sustainability

Issues of sustainability in public-private interactions are several. They include the sustainability of the initiatives themselves and that of their approaches, funding and results. In recent years, new initiatives have mushroomed in the hope of drawing attention to a variety of health problems. Many of these initiatives, however, have quickly withered away.

In the case of GAVI, money besides the Gates Foundations' contributions has not been abundant. The Gates Foundation commitment is for five years; thereafter GAVI's funding is not certain. In general, Gates' contributions are built on a venture philanthropy model, that is, the funds are meant to serve as catalyst for a limited period of time for other funds (or until the initiative becomes self-financing). In the case of GAVI, national vaccines programmes have become substantially more expensive with the addition of newer vaccines – the costs have in places tripled (Brugha and Walt 2001). Even if the prices of new vaccines have become lower, the costs of the new programmes may still be financially unsustainable in the longer term. GFATM, meanwhile, has been unable to attract private sector resources; indeed, it has not been able to gather as many resources as it stated it needed. It has not been able to attract new contributions and many of the initial pledges have already been granted in funds to projects.

All programmes with short-term funding risk being unsustainable. In the case of PPPs, there are greater dangers: a weak organisational backing and unclear structures of public accountability means that there may be less commitment from the public sector towards the goals of the PPPs. PPPs are described, however, as being more efficient than public sector programmes. This perception seems to depend on an understanding of efficiency as efficient transfer of money, which leads to large grants. It may, however, also lead to expensive and unsustainable solutions that may exceed the absorption capacity of the recipient.

Sustainable results usually require sustainable policies, structures and approaches. For example with the demands concerning efficiency, GAVI and GFATM felt pressurised to start functioning prior to having worked out the necessary policies and procedures. Vertical approaches are often prone to create their own vertical structures with insufficient integration to the existing structures. In case of GFATM there have been demands on the part US administration to set new delivery systems instead of those of the UN and the World Bank (Phillips 2002). This not only undermines the UN agencies and their delivery systems as such; it also builds up new structures that may not be supported or sustained in the long-term. GAVI has not paid adequate attention to strengthening existing immunization systems (although it has recently began to rectify this omission). When GAVI funding stops, however, country may well be left with the same immunisation infrastructure that it had before GAVI, but with higher expectations of the range of vaccines that could be delivered. Vaccine coverage, like HIV/AIDS treatment, needs to be sustained for their benefits to be continued.

5.6 The UN's organizational modes of functioning

Private sector involvement with UN agencies may have significant effects on the ways in which UN organisations work. The first issue of serious concern is that GHPPPs, and other new organizational structures for health-related development aid that circumvent the UN, are competing for the same funding resources as the UN. This therefore threatens the financial sustainability of UN systems. Furthermore, the relevance of the UN in critical global public health matters is being undermined by removing essential health policy issues from its auspices and fragmenting them among various PPPs. The time and effort that UN staff provide in building up the GHPPPs policies, mechanisms and procedures and in evaluating individual countries at various points in the project cycle detracts from the other work they should be doing as UN staff.

Some UN agencies, such as WHO and Unicef, have been successful in attracting corporate money. It is important, however, that these organizations do not become reliant on corporate money and lose their independence. Although reliance of just one source is also problematic if that source is voluntary contributions from governments, foundations and the corporate sector tend to be more precise and directive on the policies and programmes they would like to see in the agencies. Some foundations are such big donors that they can potentially have a significant say in policies and programmes. Anecdotes on both WHO and Unicef indicate that it is believed that such pressures have had an impact on policies. Such beliefs, whether true or not, can damage the image of UN organisations as impartial bodies.

PPPs may have a positive effect of simplifying procedures and accelerating the speed by with which decisions and actions are taken at UN structures. But the UN agencies should work closely with their governing bodies and member states in all matters that are highly relevant to policy. The demands for business-like efficiency in decision-making and action do not always mesh will with intergovernmental consensus building. In this context, issues of extreme relevance to policy may be reduced to technical matters, particularly in situations in which potential conflicts of interest have not been properly worked out. Furthermore, demands for results-based monitoring do not fit well with intersectoral action for health nor with horizontal policies and normative functions.

Business involvement seems to decrease transparency in UN agencies and their sense of direct public accountability but to increase the sense of accountability to the corporate partners. One striking example of this lack of transparency is the secrecy surrounding Unicef's guidelines and instructions for its staff on interactions with the private sector and surrounding its corporate screening criteria. The agency has not responded to most of the numerous requests to receive a copy of the guidelines. The director of Unicef's Private Sector Division justified this policy by citing the need to be careful with business partners. To allow public scrutiny, the basis of agreements between UN agencies, programmes or funds and the corporate sector should be made public. A lack of transparency in PPPs and in internal discussions within PPPs hampers public scrutiny to ensure that public interests are respected.

The lines of public accountability in GHPPPs are somewhat unclear and at best complicated. The accountability of UN agencies to their own governing bodies is problematic in structures which imply shared decision-making, especially when there is a lack of full transparency. When the WHO's Executive Board endorsed WHO's involvement in GAVI (EB/105.R4), it highlighted improving access to sustainable immunization systems, expanding the use of all existing safe and cost-effective vaccines, accelerating the development and introduction of new vaccines, and directing research and development efforts to vaccines and related products specifically needed by developing countries, particularly vaccines against for HIV/AIDS, malaria and tuberculosis. In practice, however, GAVI has focused on introducing new vaccines and given less emphasis to building sustainable systems and providing basic vaccines. Its research-funding arm has not yet been opened. The role of the WHO representative on GAVI's board is complicated, because her mandate differs in some respects from the direction that GAVI has taken.

5.7 Safeguards

The most important safeguard for each UN agency is that its secretariat has a clear understanding of the organisation's mandate and the public interests it is meant to pursue and defend. No guideline or code of conduct will solve the problem of conflict of interest if the organisation is not clear on this issue.

Many UN agencies have recognised the need to train their staff on private sector interactions. But of concern is that conflicts of interest have been poorly recognised, conceptualized and managed, especially when the potential conflict goes beyond the personal benefits to individuals (Mezzalama and Ouedraogo 1999). For example, the Commission of Macroeconomics and Health commissioning a report on the significance of generic pharmaceuticals from the research and development industry illustrates this lack of managing issues of conflict of interest (Boseley 2002). The WHO has planned staff training on conflicts of interest, but it has yet to materialise. The focus of the proposed training on PPPs at UNFPA, however, seems to be on how to engage in PPPs. The Unicef training has included, in addition to guidance on how to engage in PPIs and what the procedures are, guidance towards more globally uniform prices for corporations to pay for their interactions with Unicef.

Guidelines, instruments and procedures are necessary, even if not sufficient, prerequisites for adequate PPIs. The practices so far on public-private partnerships have, at times, preceded official mandates, procedures, guidelines and other tools to guide these developments, although the UN agencies have now developed, or are in the process of doing so, guidelines and procedures for interactions with the private sector.

Five UN agencies are also in the process of developing a common corporate assessment tool, which will focus in principle on a simplified list of Global Compact principles. The UN agencies should assess the corporations they engage with very carefully. A corporate partner's negative reputation can easily damage the UN's reputation. When GAIN was launched, it included several corporations clearly unsuitable for the UN to partner with: one was linked to a tobacco company, another has been accused of breaking the code on marketing infant formula. Although these inclusions now seem to have been dropped in more recent communications from GAIN, it is not clear how these corporations were approved in the first place.

Assessments of the risks and benefits of these partnerships tend to focus on the risks for the public image of the UN agency, programme or fund and on the immediate benefits of the PPP. Evaluating the risks and benefits in a broader framework and longer time frame is much more difficult. The guidelines and procedures which have been drawn up do not address the monitoring of PPPs, nor to they discuss criteria for dissolving the PPPs.

Another fundamental principle is the organisations' transparency about their relationships with the corporate sector and the principles that guide these relationships. The current lack of transparency threatens their public accountability.

While the WHO has its own governing bodies, the UN Funds are directed by the policies of the General Assembly and guidance from the UN's Economic and Social Council (ECOSOC). The role of the various Executive Boards of the UN Funds is, among others, to implement the policies formulated at the General Assembly, and the coordination and guidance received from the Council. They also give guidance to the head of the Fund on the Fund's work (GA A/RES/48/162) and decide on administrative and financial plans and budgets. From the interviews, it seems that the role of these Executive Boards could be strengthened to ensure the democratic accountability of the various Funds. A prerequisite for the proper role of the Executive Boards is that they receive the relevant documents, such as the guidelines on PPPs, to review and that they are consulted on decisions of major policy-relevance – and their comments acted upon.

5.8 Undue advantage

The current popular phrase, a "win-win situation", to describe an arrangement such as a PPP in which everybody is believed to benefit provides little or no ground for openly weighing up the pros and cons of the arrangement and little unbiased analysis on "who wins what". A major reason given for the corporation interest in forming PPPs has been their corporate responsibility, although corporations should not need the reward of the UN prestige to behave responsibly.

While business interests rights and gains are not the focus of this paper, one might ask whether it is fair to give some companies the advantage of UN prestige and not their competitors. Current initiatives favour large transnational companies over small and medium size ones, in contrast to New Economic Order initiatives of the 1970s (*see also* Utting 2000). Although no official policy exists, interview data suggests that the Global Compact is not very interested in small companies in practice. Unicef is more interested in market leaders as their partners. UNFPA collaborations with contraceptive producers were focused on major transnational companies, which were asked to name the countries in which they would like to gain new or further markets (UNFPA 1999). Similarly, WHO's dialogue initiatives centre on major companies rather than on smaller local producers.

Both the UN general guidelines on interacting with the corporate sector, as well as the policies of the individual UN agencies, state that no exclusive rights should be given to any one company nor does the agency or the UN endorse the products of the companies with which they partner. But not all corporations can get "partnerships" with the UN. If the amount of money the company pays is a critical factor in the "partnership" or alliance, then only richer and bigger companies will be candidates.

6. Recommendations for Finland and like-minded countries

6.1 Funding

It is important to ensure an adequate resource base for the UN system, preferably in the form of longer-term commitments. In principle, core funding with little earmarking, combined with a strong input in the official governing bodies, would be the most democratic way of allocating resources and influencing policies. In the past, Finland has given the WHO fairly low levels of earmarked funding and much higher levels of core funding to Unicef and UNFPA. This practice tradition has been grounded in the Nordic policy project which argues that WHO, as a specialized agency, should concentrate on normative functions which need relatively few resources while the UN Funds which implement programmes mainly in the developing countries need considerably more resources. There might be a need to elaborate this thinking, however, since WHO's normative tasks also need resources and other input at all levels, including at national levels, even though WHO should not turn itself into a development agency. The issue of earmarking versus core funding is a complicated one. Finland might need to reassess its core funding provided with little input into decision-making structures in the light of increased corporate influence which has been linked with pressures from some member states, foundations and the corporate sector itself. At the same time, there is currently much less pressure from donors on the UN agencies to be more cautious about their interactions with the corporate sector. Finland and other like-minded countries should advocate that the UN agencies take the utmost care in their corporate relationships in terms of screening the corporations, assessing the content of the proposed interactions and selecting the form of interaction that is most advantageous for the UN's goals and the least risky to the UN's integrity. They should also advocate that UN agencies plan their activities at levels such that they do not become dependent on corporate funding.

Finland has so far not decided to give funding to any GHPPP. In general, GHPPPs are meant to attract money that is in addition to existing development aid. Thus Finnish policy follows the original conception that GHPPPs should not divert funding away from existing channels and organisations. The GHPPPs are organised in such a way as to be able to accept funding in a limited timeframe and with little trouble for the donor. Finland should therefore consider what its position on the several GHPPPs might be should it find some additional and unexpected resources. Such decisions, however, should be based on due deliberations over the advantages and achievements of the particular GHPPP. To date, the functioning GHPPPs have not presented sufficient evidence to justify their funding and there are grave concerns about their governance structure – the inclusion of corporations with vested interests in their decision-making bodies and the lack of clarity on public accountability – that need to be addressed (discussed further below).

Scrutiny over interactions between the UN and the private sector should certainly not be left to the NGO community. But it would be wise to ensure that NGOs and academic institutions which do monitor corporate behaviour and PPIs have adequate resources for their work, work that is used as a resource by official screening procedures, including some UN procedures. Finland might want to consider providing funding for such entities to continue and strengthen their valuable work.

6.2 Policies

Finland and like-minded countries need to take an active part in policy-making within the UN system. This implies active participation in EU discussions on UN policies; articulating Finnish positions on the various UN agencies in cases where the EU is not required to speak in a common voice; and providing adequate resources to participate in the governing bodies of the various agencies.

While interactions with the private sector are both necessary and, in their proper forms, desirable, Finland, perhaps with some like-minded countries, could advocate an assessment of the PPPs and PPIs within the UN and of the safeguards in place to ensure UN integrity and that the public interest really remains at the core of all UN activities. It is of particular importance to develop adequate mechanisms, procedures and guidelines to ensure that corporate interests are sufficiently separated from public interests and that any conflicts between the two are dealt with transparently. The stated aim of the PPP framework to include corporations in policy-making is problematic. The utmost care should be taken that interactions with the private sector do not interfere with the normative functions of the UN bodies. In the area of health, it is especially important that the WHO keeps corporations at an adequate distance from its policy-making processes. An important perquisite for ensuring that public interests remain at the core of UN activities is that guides, procedures, mechanisms, agreements and activities are available for democratic scrutiny. Criteria for monitoring and dissolving partnerships should be developed. Finland should insist on transparency in corporate relationships at all stages.

The Finnish government has actively participated in formulating and following the contents of WHO's policies and practices, but has provided comparably less input to the policy issues of the UN Funds. In the future, while its active role in WHO policy-making should continue, Finland should consider playing a more active role in UN Funds as well. This active participation could include ensuring that the policies adopted by UN agencies strengthen the integrity of the UN and are guided by the public interest of the world's peoples. The role of the Executive Boards of the various UN Funds should be strengthened so as to ensure that they can give guidance about implementing the policies adopted by the UN's General Assembly. A necessary prerequisite of this is that the Executive Boards must review issues that are highly relevant to policies, such as issues related to private sector interactions. Such follow-up and monitoring requires adequate staff resources, as well as close collaboration between the various sectors at the national level, to ensure that the relevant sectoral issues are properly considered.

The health-related work of the UN should be guided by long-term horizontal policies and values endorsed by the UN system, such as the "Health For All" policy. There are currently concerns that horizontal policies are being overridden by global vertical technological solutions. This policy direction is not caused solely by the PPIs, but is prompted by them. It is also important that policy-making on essential public health matters remains within the auspices of the UN and is not divided up among various structures outside the UN. Such fragmenting is detrimental not only at the global level, but also and in particular for national health policy-making. Finland should urge that renewed emphasis is placed on the development of nationally driven health policies and systems.

Policies in line with Finnish development policies should ensure that proper needs assessments of the receiving countries form the basis of foreign development assistance. A country's needs should not be overridden by fixed predetermined solutions designed at the global level in a framework that resembles that of the GHPPPs. Efforts should be made to ensure that these international inputs are integrated with ongoing processes within countries, such as sector-wide approaches and drawing up poverty reduction strategy papers (PRSPs).

It is also important to ensure that industrial policies in the North do not override health policies. This means that health policies, programmes and interventions are selected without considering Northern industrial policy aims or financial goals, and that the flexibilities in the WTO's trade-related intellectual property rights agreement are not restricted or undermined. Such processes should not be enhanced by having vested industries in policy-making positions. The viability of the healthy traditions, including in the area of nutrition, should be nourished. When technological and industrial solutions are appropriate, however, the viability of the relevant national or regional industries should not be harmed by the UN's increased collaboration with the large, often transnational companies.

Acknowledgements

I should like to thank Dr. Judith Richter for researching some of the issues explored in this paper, for suggesting contacts, and for sharing invaluable material, insights and thoughts on UN-business partnerships from a public interest perspective. I am also indebted to the GASPP information officer, Minna Ilva, for literature searches, for planning and collating the Annex, and for compiling the figures. Professor Bob Deacon and Dr. Meri Koivusalo provided valuable comments on a draft version of this paper. Sarah Sexton edited the text. I thank them all for their comments, advice and help in preparing this paper. Nevertheless, the contents remain my responsibility alone.

References

Annan, K. (1997), *Secretary-general, in address to World Economic Forum, stresses strengthened partnership between United nations, private sector,* UN Press release SG/SM/6153.

Annan, K. (1999), " A Compact for the New Century", Address to the World Economic Forum, Davos Switzerland, 31 January 1999.

Bellamy, C. (1999), Statement of UNICEF Executive Director Carol Bellamy to Harvard International Development Conference on 'sharing responsibilites: public, private & civil society', 16 April 1999, UNICEF, [online] available: http://www.un.org/partners/business/unicef14.htm.

Bellamy, C. (2002), Letter addressed to Mr. Ruskin, 13 August 2002. UNICEF.

Boseley, S. (2002), Unhealthy influence. There is a donages that WHO's new partnership with drug companies will skew its health policies, *The Guardian* 6 February, 2002 .

Brugha, R. and Walt, G. (2001), "A global health fund: aleap of faith," *British medical Journal,* vol. 323, pp. 152–4.

Brundtland, G. H. (1998), "Dr Gro Harlem Brundtland Director-General Elect The World Health Organization". Speech to the Fifty-first World Health Assembly Geneva, 13 May 1998, WHO, A51/DIV/6.

Brundtland, G. H. (2001), "Remarks to the meeting of the Governors of the Health Industry", Speech of the Director-General of WHO in World Economic Froum, 29 January 2001, Davos, Switzerland.

Buse, K. and Walt, G. (2000), "Global public-private partnerships for health: part I – a new development in health," *Bulletin of the World Health Organization – The International Journal of Public Health,* vol. 78, no.4, pp. 549–561.

Buse, K. and Waxman, A. (2001), "Public-Private health partnerships: a strategy for WHO," *Bulletin of the World Health Organization,* vol. 79, no. 4, pp. 748–754.

Commission on macroeconomics and health (2001), *Macroeconomics and health: investing in health for economic development. Report of the commission on macroeconomics and health,* World Health Organization, Geneva.

Essential Information (2002), "Unicef and McDonald's World Children's Day", 26 August 2002, [online] available: http://www.globalpolicy.org/reform/business/2002/unicefandmcd.htm

Ferriman, A. (2000), "WHO accused of stifling debate on infant feeding," *British Medical Journal,* vol. 320, p. 1362.

Freedman, A. M. and Stecklow, S. (2000), "Unicef vs. baby-formula industry: the dispute begins to spill over", *Wall Street Journal,* 5 December 2000.

Gellman, B. (2000), "A turning point that left millions behind", *Washington Post,* 27 December 2000, A01.

Hardon, A. (2000), "'Immunization for all? A critical look at the first GAVI partners meeting," *HAI-Lights,* vol. 6, no. 1, pp. 2–9.

Hayes, L. (2001), "Industry's growing influence at the WHO", *Health Action International,* 15 December 2001.

Jarrett, S. (2002), *Vaccination Financing Conference Presentation on Vaccine Security,* Cape Town, 11 April 2002.

Jenkins, R. (2001), *Corporate Codes of Conduct. Self regulating in a global economy.* UNRISD, Geneva.

Kickbush, I. and Quick, J. (1998), "Partnerships for health in the 21st century", *World Health Statistics Quarterly,* vol. 58, pp. 68–74.

Kopp, C. (2000), "WHO industry partnership on the hot seat," *British Medical Journal,* vol. 321.

Korten, D. (1997), "The United Nations and the corporate agenda, *UN Reform,*" [internet circulation], available: www.globalpolicy.org/reform/korten.htm.

McNeil, D. (2002), "U.N. Disease Fund Opens Way to Generics" *The New York Times,* 16 October 2002.

Mezzalama, F. and Ouedraogo, L. D. (1999), *Private sector involvement and cooperation with the United Nations system,* Joint Inspection Unit, United Nations, Geneva.

Motchane, J.-L. (2002), "Health for all or riches for some. WHO's responsible?", *Le Monde Diplomatique,* 17 July 2002.

Muraskin, W. (2002), The last years of the CVI and the birth of the GAVI, in: Reich, M. R. (ed) *Public-private partnerships for public health,* Harvard Center for Population and Development Studies, Cambrigde, Massachusetts, pp. 115–68.

Nelson, J. (2002), *Building partnerships. Cooperation between the United Nations and the private sector,* Department of Public Information, United Nations, New York.

Pear, R. and Oppel, R. A. (2002), "Drug industry seeks ways to capitalize on election success," *New York Times,* 21 November , Politics.

Phillips, M. (2002), "Infectious-disease fund stalls amid U.S. rules for disbursal," *Wall Street Journal,* 5 August 2002 .

Richter, J. (2000a), *Holding Corporations Accountable: Corporate Conduct, International Codes and Citizen Action,* Zed Books, London and New York.

Richter, J. (2000b), "A question of standards?", *British Medical Journal,* vol. 321, pp. 956.

Ruskin, Gary (2002), "Coalition asks UNICEF to cancel "McDonald's World Children's Day". *Commercial Alert,* 31 July 2002. [online] available: http://www.commondreams.org/news2002/ 0731-02.htm, (accessed 6 Dec 2002).

Sokol, E. (2000), "Changes to paper served to stifle debate," *British Medical Journal,* vol. 321, p. 956.

Starling, M., Burgha, R. and Walt, G. (2001), *New products into old systems. The initial impact of the Global Alliance for Vaccines and Immunization (GAVI) at country level,* London School of Hygiene and Tropical Medicine and Save the Children, UK, London.

Tesner, S. with Kell, W. G. (2000), *The United Nations and business. A partnership recovered,* St. Martin's Press, New York.

UNFPA, (1999), *The UNFPA Private-sector initiative. Exploring ways to facilitate cooperation between governments and the commercial sector to expand access to reproductive health commodities,* Technical and Policy Division, UNFPA, New York.

UNICEF (1995), *UNICEF Annual Report,* UNICEF, New York.

United Nations (1994), *Report of the international conference on population and development,* United Nations, A/conf.171/13.

Utting, P. (2000), "UN-Business Partnerships: Whose Agenda Counts?" In conference: *Partnerships for Development or Privatization of the Multilateral System?* North-South Coalition, Oslo, Norway.

Vaughan, P.J. et al (1995), *Cooperation for health development. Extrabudgetary funds in the World Health Organisation.* May 1995, Australian Agency for International Development, Royal Ministry of Foreign Affairs, Norway, Overseas Development Administration, UK.

Verheul, E. and Rowson, M. (2001), "Poverty reduction strategy papers", *British Medical Journal,* vol. 323, pp. 120–1.

Vidal, J. (1997), *McLibel. Burger culture on trial,* Pan Books, London.

Yamey, G. (2002), "WHO in 2002. Faltering steps towards partnerships", *British Medical Journal,* vol. 325, pp. 1236–40.

Zeltner, T., Kessler, D. A., Martiny, A. and Randera, F. (2000), *Tobacco company strategies to undermine tobacco control activities at the World Health Organization. Report of the committee of experts on tobacco industry documents,* [online] available: http://www.who.int.

Zimmerman, R. (2002), "Gates fights malnutrition with cheese, ketchup and other fortified food items", *Wall Street Journal,* 9 May 2002 .

ANNEX 1   Review of Guidelines

GUIDELINES	Cooperation between the United Nations and the Business Community[1]	UNICEF Guidelines and Manual for Working with the Business Community[2]	WHO Guidelines on interaction with commercial enterprises to achieve health outcomes[3]
Purpose and Rationale	– Facilitate the formulation and implementation of cooperation – Ensure the integrity of the Organization – Serve as a common framework for all organizations of the UN proper (= UN Secretariat, UN funds and programmes)	– Business community has an important influence on the lives of children and families. – Collaborating with business can bring significant resources to improve children's lives	To help WHO staff to interact appropriately with commercial enterprises in order to achieve positive outcomes for health.
Definition	Business defined as for-profit enterprises		Commercial enterprises are defined as businesses that are intended to make a profit for their owners. Some or all of these guidelines can also apply to a variety of other institutions including State-run enterprises, associations representing commercial enterprises, foundations not at arms length from their sponsors, and other not-for-profit organizations such as academic institutions
General Principles	– advance UN goals as laid in the Charter – clear delineation of roles and responsibilities – maintain integrity and independence of UN – no unfair advantage – transparency of cooperation	UNICEF actively seeks alliance with those in the business community: – whose behaviour demonstrates a willingness to exercise Corporate Social responsibility. – who demonstrate a commitment to UNICEF's mandate and core values. Two Guiding Principles: 1) find the best ally : corporate assessment ; measured against Unicef fundamental principles 2) find the best alliance: fit with Unicef's values, mission, mandate and brand values –> No endorsement –> No exclusivity	The main objective of the interaction is to further WHO's mission and policies. (a) the relationship should contribute to improving public health; (b) the public health gains should be commensurate with the time and expense involved in establishing and maintaining the relationship; (c) relationships should be established on the basis of an exchange of clearly written letters or agreements indicating the contribution (financial or otherwise) that each of the parties brings to the relationship.
Authorization (use of name and emblem)	The UN Office of Legal Affairs	Alliance to be reviewed and approved by Co-ordination Committee	Office of the Legal Counsel should be consulted

---

[1] United Nations (2000), *Guidelines for cooperation between the United Nations and the business community,* Issued by the Secretary-General 17 July 2000.
[2] Unicef (2001), *Building Alliances for Children, UNICEF Guidelines and Manual for Working with the Business Community, Summary.*
[3] World Health Organization (2000), *Guidelines on interaction with commercial enterprise to achieve health outcomes,* 30 November 2000, Document EB107/20, Annex.

GUIDELINES	Cooperation between the United Nations and the Business Community	UNICEF Guidelines and Manual for Working with the Business Community	WHO Guidelines on working with the private sector to achieve health outcomes
Types of interaction	Cooperation with business can take many forms, such as: – advocacy – fund-raising – policy dialogue – humanitarian assistance – development cooperation	Alliance with the business community – programmatic alliances – advocacy – fundraising support – contributions-in-kind	WHO interactions with commercial enterprises include: – participation with one or more commercial enterprises in alliances and other relationships to address specific health issues – exchange of information – product research and development aimed at improving health
Modalities/ forms of partnership	– direct contribution by the business partner – indirect contribution through the establishment of a charitable organization or foundation – partnership in technical assistance projects – partnership in promoting the purposes and activities of the UN – partnership in cooperative projects		– generation of cash and in-kind donations to WHO – advocacy for health – donations (with particular attention given to avoiding real or perceived conflicts of interest) – contributions in kind – product development – seconded personnel – use of WHO name and logo – organization or sponsoring of meetings

GUIDELINES	Cooperation between the United Nations and the Business Community	UNICEF Guidelines and Manual for Working with the Business Community	WHO Guidelines on working with the private sector to achieve health outcomes
Choosing a Partner **a) Criteria for Partnerships** **b) Exclusion criteria**	Global Compact principles as a reference point a) Business partners should demonstrate responsible citizenship by supporting UN causes and core values as reflected in the Charter and other relevant conventions and treaties. Within their sphere of influence, private enterprises should have demonstrated a commitment to meeting or exceeding the principles of the Compact by translating them into operational corporate practice. b)Business entities that are complicit in human rights abuses, tolerate forced or compulsory labour or the use of child labour, are involved in the sale or manufacture of anti-personnel mines or their components, or that otherwise do not meet relevant obligations or responsibilities by the United Nations, are not eligible for partnership.	a) Alliances with entities that display corporate social responsibility and leadership in the community; make a positive contribution to society; have a record of socially-responsible behaviour; have a positive public and/or product/ service image; have a history of commitment to development-related causes; have responsible labour practices; and employ responsible environmental practices. b) No alliances are possible with businesses in the armaments and weapons sector; toy manufacturers manufacturing replica weapons marketed to children; alcohol or tobacco companies; companies which violate United Nations sanctions; manufacturers of infant formula whose marketing practices violate the International Code for Marketing of Breastmilk Substitutes; and companies involved in pornography, exploitative and/or corrupt practices; companies found in violation of environmental laws.	a)Commercial enterprises working with WHO will be expected to conform to WHO public health policies in the areas of food safety, chemical safety, ethical promotion of medicinal drug products, tobacco control, and others In addition, evaluation criteria should be applied which are similar to those already in use by a range of public agencies in assessing potential partnerships with commercial enterprises, including: the public image, and financial stability and integrity of the company. Specific criteria for donations in cash, contributions in kind, secondments, product development, cost recovery, meetings, hospitality b) Relationships should be avoided with commercial enterprises whose activities are incompatible with WHO's work, such as the tobacco or arms industries. WHO should avoid indirect collaboration (particularly if arranged by a third party acting as an intermediary between WHO and a commercial enterprise).
Procedures		All potential alliances are to be subjected to the "Best Ally, Best Alliance" review as a matter of course. UNICEF's *Private Sector Division (International Accounts Section)* is the organization's focal point to provide guidance in this area – including in connection with the initial corporate screening or "due diligence". Where the alliance would involve using the UNICEF name, logo or emblem in commercial context, especially in fundraising alliances, it is to be reviewed by a *Co-Ordination Committee*, established by Executive Director. (Also in alliances which require further consideration).	The *Office of the Legal Counsel* will review the proposal and if, in the Office's opinion, there is no conflict of interest, the proposed arrangement will be cleared for action. If, in the opinion of the Office of the Legal Counsel, there is doubt as to whether the interaction is acceptable under the guidelines, the Office of the Legal Counsel will, in consultation with the programme concerned, submit the proposed arrangement to the *Committee on Private Sector Collaboration*.

III
THE IMPACT OF WTO AGREEMENTS ON HEALTH AND DEVELOPMENT POLICIES

Meri Koivusalo

Senior Researcher
Globalism and Social Policy Programme (GASPP)
STAKES

1. Summary

This policy brief will assess and analyse the role and relevance of the World Trade Organisation and trade agreements hosted by the organisation from a health policy point of view with attention to matters of special importance of developing countries as well as to those where interests of developing countries and developed countries may be in conflict. The brief first sets the background in providing some information and views on trade and development matters and the role of World Trade Organisation as well as on health and health policy issues in the context of global trade policies. The brief then goes through aspects of three main agreements and specific matters with respect to the role of the European Community.

This brief takes as granted that the dominant assumption informing trade policies is that liberalisation of trade is beneficial to health policies through economic growth and that no major conflicts exist between health and trade policies. The purpose of this brief has been to contest this basic assumption and track down and inform what could be the problems from a health policy perspective. Furthermore, it presents policy issues and perspectives mostly from a health viewpoint, which is not and cannot be the only viewpoint against which policy decisions are judged. This health viewpoint also assumes that health policy aims in the development context are based on the same values of solidarity and universality as they are at the national level.

The brief first takes up some aspects in relation to trade and development, WTO and development as well as trade and health policies in the international scene. It also shortly deals with WTO's role in order to provide background for the arguments why WTO has become important. Health is only partly determined by health sector policies; general welfare policies also have a fundamental role in people's capacities to stay healthy. However, while some reference is made to social policy matters this paper does not deal in detail on broader social policy, poverty reduction or labour issues. An appropriate analysis on these matters would require a review focussing on these broad and important policy matters. In spite of this some focus is given to food security and legal trade in substances hazardous to health due to the crucial importance of these in the developing world. The first chapter on agriculture and consumption aims to track down matters of importance with respect to trade flows in goods and their implication to consumption of nutritious food and health hazardous substances.

Trade agreements influence health and health policy options also beyond development policies and a further analysis focuses on health policy implications of trade agreements. It is argued that from a health policy perspective the interests of developing and developed countries in the sectoral health policy matters are in many cases closer than has been maintained in the context of trade policies, where arguments tend to be divided between developed and developing countries. Furthermore, where conflicts of interests between developed and developing countries can be seen, it is of importance to note that often these are not related to disagreements in health policies, but rather as result of different prioritisation.

Finally, the section on European policies deals with the challenge of reconciling health and development aims with trade policies in the European context, where the European Community is increasingly expected to speak coherently and by one voice. It is thus recognised that especially in trade matters focus needs to be laid more at European level and on European policies.

2. Background: The WTO, development and international trade

The decision to establish the World Trade Organisation (WTO) was taken in April 1994 in Marrakech, Morocco, at the completion of the eight-year "Uruguay Round" of renegotiating the General Agreement on Tariffs and Trade (GATT) (WTO 1995). The WTO is the successor to GATT, but does far more than simply continue GATT's role. It has not only a broader country membership than GATT, but also a broader coverage of commercial activities and trade policies. Indeed, it has been described as "the widest-ranging multilateral trade agreement ever negotiated" (Griesgraber and Gunter 1997). The GATT applied to international trade in merchandise goods only: the WTO covers not only cross-border trade in goods but also that in services, agriculture and ideas or "intellectual property". Unlike GATT, the WTO has an institutional foundation and WTO commitments are full and permanent (WTO 1995). The WTO has the capacity to enforce its rules through its dispute settlement process, a power that other UN agencies, such as the WHO or ILO, do not have and that also GATT lacked. It has thus been claimed that the global regulation of trade by bodies such as the WTO implies a significant renegotiation of the Westphalian notion of state sovereignty (Held et al 1999).

The WTO is based in Geneva, Switzerland. On 1st January 1995, 76 countries became members of the WTO (WTO 1998a). The membership has since grown to 144 countries as of 1 January 2002 (WTO 2002). The WTO's highest authority is the Ministerial Conference, a meeting of representatives of WTO member countries which has to take place at least every two years. The day-to-day work of the WTO falls to a number of subsidiary bodies, primarily the General Council that reports to the Ministerial Conference. Development issues are also dealt with in the Trade and Development Committee and its subcommittee on Least Developed Countries. (WTO 2002) The United Nations Conference on Trade and Development (UNCTAD) has also a specific remit to focus on trade and development (UNCTAD 2002a).

Linkages between international financial and trade institutions have become closer and more complex than ever (Ahn 2000). It seems that trade proponents and the development community have kind of chosen to work more closely with the more donor dominated World Bank and the OECD (Organisation of Economic Cooperation and Development) on matters of development and trade. This does not seem to be unrelated with the fact that current agenda of the World Bank and the OECD is directed towards deepening and extending trade liberalisation, while UNCTAD has placed more emphasis on development matters. This has direct implications to the interests of developing countries and has raised concern also amongst NGOs, which have criticised the World Banks role in capacity building in trade and development in the developing countries (*see* e.g. www.brettonwoodsproject.org).

The underlying philosophy of the WTO is that open markets, non-discrimination between country trading partners, and global competition in international trade are conducive to the national welfare of all countries (Hoekman and Kostecki 1995). There has been considerable debate in recent years about the overall benefits to developing countries of increased international trade and further integration with the global economy. The costs to developing countries of implementing the Uruguay Round have also been discussed. According to the World Bank calculations the implementation costs could imply around 130 US $million – most probably even more – to a country. The costs of implementation of only three of the agreements represent the magnitude of the annual development budgets of many least developed countries (Finger and Schuler 1999). In terms of international trade, the least developed countries, with 10 % of world population, account for just 0.3% of world trade, half their share of two decades ago (UNDP 1997).

The share of least developed countries in world exports of goods and services declined by 47% between 1980 and 1999 (UNCTAD 2002b). Foreign investment, frequently cited as the engine of economic growth, takes place mostly between North America,

Europe and Japan. Together with China, these areas receive more than 90% of all foreign direct investments. The rest of the world, with 70% of the world's people, receives less than 10% (UNDP 1997). The share of multinational corporations in global trade has been growing is expected to increase still further. Intra-company trade now accounts for an estimated 40% of world trade (Cook and Kirkpatrick 1995). Primary commodities still seem to account for the majority of exports for developing countries and even in the case of increasing exports in manufactured goods it seems that developing countries seem to be engaged with lower profitability and more basic exports thus not being able to reap the expected gains from exports of manufactured goods. Between 1997 and 2001 copper prices fell by 27%, cotton prices by 39% and coffee prices by 66% (UNCTAD 2002b)

This inequality between the developed and developing worlds has been reflected in both the nature of the Uruguay Round negotiations and in the resulting agreements, particularly those covering agriculture, textiles and intellectual property rights (see e.g. Stewart 1995; Khor 1999; Third World Network 2001; Rodrik 2001). The current process of globalisation has been uneven in terms of trade and investments (Hirst and Thompson 1996), and runs the risk of marginalising still further the poorest nations. But the terms under which developing countries integrate further with the world economy are also of concern. Attention has been drawn, for example, to the nature and requirements of foreign direct investments as well as to their costs and risks (South Centre 1997a).

It is difficult to ensure that the process of single undertaking in WTO trade negotiations serve the very different interests of developing countries. Likewise for health concerns. During the Uruguay Round, for instance, developing countries were reluctant to approve the Agreement on Trade-Related Aspects of Intellectual Property Rights (TRIPS), but it was sold to them as part of the more general package of WTO agreements (CIPR 2002; Haaparanta 2001, Third World Network 2001). The World Bank has previously raised the issue of intellectual property rights and has encouraged developing countries to ensure that their interests are served when trade-related intellectual property rights are discussed (World Bank 1998, Butler 1998a). However, the practice of pressure and power politics has nothing but continued as in the Doha Ministerial, the adoption of public health declaration has been claimed to be used directly to pressure developing countries to accept inclusion of new issues (Kwa 2002).

The World Trade Organisation prefers to define itself as a system of rules dedicated to open, fair and undistorted competition (WTO 1995). In the WTO context fairness is primarily considered as fairness between treatment of national and foreign products and services. This would imply equal treatment to small-scale farmers and multinational companies. Powerful multinational actors and transnational corporations complicate trade policies and negotiations and many of them exceed the economic strength of nation states. Moreover, WTO member countries are at different stages of industrialisation and have different capacities to benefit from trade openness.

The WTO dispute settlement system is closed and while only countries may appeal, the process of dispute settlement does eventually lead to both the development and interpretation of international case law. The dispute settlement process has no obligatory public health consultation and the expertise of panels is limited to senior trade figures (Understanding 1994). This means that any case law relating to the trade restrictiveness of public health policy measures will be adjudicated by senior trade officials and not by public health experts. The WTO dispute settlement process and its implications to scope of public policies governments can undertake also clearly points problems of the current practices (Correa 2000). The functions of the dispute settlement system are problematic also from the development perspective. While the WTO's dispute settlement system does allow all WTO member countries to appeal against another member's practices that they believe contravene the WTO rules. But it is clear that any resulting trade sanctions imposed by Burkina Faso on the United States and EU, for instance, have much less impact than those imposed by the US and EU on Burkina Faso. It has also become clear that the dispute settlement process itself is not cheap. It requires a country to commit resources of time, money and experienced people, making it more difficult for poorer and smaller nations to use it compared to richer and larger countries.

The claim that the involvement of various transnational policy actors in the WTO process has created a democratic deficit relates to their involvement in negotiations and follow up of the implementation of the resulting agreements. Business interests are often articulated through relevant governments, at times very directly. The Cargill Corporation,[1] for instance, epitomised the role that multinational corporations played in the Uruguay Round of GATT negotiations, which concluded with the WTO's establishment. The United States proposal for a multilateral agricultural agreement was written by a Cargill senior executive, while Cargill employees on the US official delegation led the US negotiations throughout the Reagan, Bush and Clinton presidencies (Kneen 1995, van der Stichele 1998).

Another example of the importance of corporate actors in designing and negotiation of a WTO agreement is the WTO's TRIPS Agreement (Agreement on Trade-related 1994). The TRIPS agreement did not result from all countries weighing up the various options and choosing the best, but rather from the lobbying power and rent seeking of the international corporate sector, and especially research-based pharmaceutical industry

---

[1] Cargill is the largest private corporation in the North America producing, processing and trading in agricultural commodities.

(see e.g. Drahos 1995; Drahos 1997). At the 1997 Ministerial Conference held in Singapore, most of the non-governmental organisations present were business-related organisations (Marceau and Pedersen 1999).

It is clear that the meaning of civil society changed in the WTO context after the Seattle Ministerial meeting. In comparison to the business, it is clear that before and in Seattle environmental, development and public interest NGOs felt hardship in getting access to relevant information. The continuation of problematic and undemocratic processes, which act against developing countries, have been documented also from the Doha Ministerial calling for improvement in decision-making processes of the WTO (Kwa 2002, Third World Network 2001).

2.1 International trade and poverty reduction

The emphasis on the importance of trade liberalisation to poverty reduction is part of the guiding framework of analysis of the new World Bank trade and development handbook intended to be widely used as a reference (English et al. 2002). This assessment is clearly based on the assumption that economic growth helps to alleviate poverty (and not exacerbate it) and that the mechanism to reduce poverty is through devising and implementing anti-poverty policies, not by reforming trade policies. This is reflected also in the contribution on poverty and trade (Winters 2002)

"Trade liberalisation may have adverse consequences for some – including some poor people –that should be avoided or ameliorated to the greatest extent possible. My fundamental belief, however, is that trade liberalisation aids growth, which in turn aids poverty alleviation. I also believe that a widespread reform will contain enough positive elements so that, in general, only a few people will end up as net losers. Trade policy should therefore generally not be closely manipulated with an eye to its direct poverty consequences. It should rather, be set on a sound basis overall, with recognition that some modification may be inevitable for political and other reasons. The primary way to deal with poverty is through general antipoverty policies."

This view is based on an understanding that social policies are residual, that is, that markets dominate and poverty programmes pick up the pieces. However, it is necessary to note that in practice it also reiterates a rather neo-liberal approach to social policies and ignores in principle redistributional matters or more fundamental linkages between economic and social policy priorities. These premises also run into problems when conflicts of interest in the implications of trade agreements are discussed: in a framework pursuing the least trade restrictive and the most residual social policy, there are no real conflicts. Thus, this 'no conflicts' assumption also easily prescribes a specific type of policies as a starting point leading easily to more commercialised, costly and individualised approaches if trade.

Others have argued that while poverty reduction needs to be associated with growth, there is no convincing evidence that trade liberalisation is predictably associated with subsequent economic growth. The problem is not trade liberalisation per se, but the diversion of financial resources and political capital from more urgent development priorities. (Rodrik 2001)

The current UNCTAD view challenges the mainstream argument that a major reason why poverty exists in least developed countries is due to their low level of trade integration and insufficient trade liberalisation as grossly simplistic. According to UNCTAD the persistence of generalised poverty is less related to a lower level of integration into the global economy, and to insufficient trade liberalisation, than to the form of trade integration. However, international trade is of major importance to LDC economies. During 1997–1998 exports and imports of goods and services constituted on average 43% of their GDP. While benefits of trade liberalisation in poverty reduction has been promoted by recent analyses by the World Bank, the UNCTAD view has challenged this pointing out that rapid and deep trade liberalisation has been associated, at least in short run, with a rising incidence of poverty (UNCTAD 2002b).

2.2 International trade and health

Health is not a new issue on the international trade agenda. It was included in the GATT agreement governing international trade in goods in the form of Article XX outlining a general public health exception: (GATT 1994)

The XX Article of GATT

Subject to the requirement that such measures are not applied in a manner which would constitute a means of arbitrary or unjustifiable discrimination between countries where the same conditions prevail, or a disguised restriction on international trade, nothing in this Agreement shall be construed to prevent the adoption or enforcement by any contracting party of measures:

a) necessary to protect public morals

b) necessary to protect human, animal or plant life or health

e) relating to the products of prison labour;

International health regulations hosted by the WHO are also a result of trade and health related concerns and measures, with the aim of ensure maximum security against the international spread of diseases with minimum interference with world traffic (WHO 1999). The completion of the Uruguay Round and the establishment of the WTO added to the Article XX reference to the Agreement on the Application of Sanitary and Phytosanitary Measures (SPS) (Agreement on application 1994), as means to ensure that measures are not applied in a manner which would constitute a means of arbitrary or unjustifiable discrimination between countries where the same conditions prevail.

International health regulations and measures have a long history with trade matters in protecting the public's health by preventing food contamination or the outbreak of disease epidemics (see e.g. Fidler 1997). However, it is likely that, as a result of increased international trade in food stuffs and related products, public health officials will not only have to contend with more food-related epidemics and issues, but they will also need to be able to track their international nature and scale better. There are also ethical dimensions in trade and health matters as trade in blood products, human body-parts or services covering transplants might raise new dilemmas. Ethical matters are also related to patentability and bioethics (see e.g. Drahos 1999, Shiva 2001)

In the field of international health, the traditional forum to address health concerns has been the World Health Organisation (WHO) (Koivusalo and Ollila 1997). Relationships between the WTO and the WHO have alternated over the years. WHO's work on TRIPS and related issues raised initial concerns in late 1990s. The Doha declaration emphasis on the role between public health and trade can be tracked on a WHO resolution on the matter emphasising the priority of public health policies in 1998. WHO has produced several publications to help developing countries answer their questions about access to pharmaceuticals under the WTO regime. The WTO, however, has not always rated WHO highly. WHO does have an observer status within the WTO – but it is just an observer status. WHO's emphasis on access to pharmaceuticals within developing countries raised concerns within the WTO and generated a wariness that has been reflected in more recent relationships between the two organisations. In autumn 2001, an email from a senior staff member of the WTO, was leaked to the NGO community. In the email he explicitly outlined what he saw as the problems with WHO and its study on trade and health and the "unreliability" of the WHO because it was too close with actors such as the NGOs or the South Centre, which is a permanent intergovernmental organisation of developing countries (Palmedo 2001). It was not surprising, that the debated WHO study on the health implications of international trade agreements eventually became a joint WTO/WHO study on trade and health and reflected WTO viewpoints on health and trade more strongly than those of WHO (WTO/WHO 2002). On the other hand the Essential Drugs and Medicines Policy department has continued collaboration with the South Centre and jointly published a report on another potentially inflammable area of protection of data submitted for the registration of pharmaceuticals (Correa 2002b).

The TRIPS agreement has raised concern also amongst those who would otherwise promote free trade as many see it as means to increase monopoly power globally. There are concerns about the TRIPS agreement in most UN development agencies. While the World Bank trade-related actors would promote TRIPS, those working on health often agree that TRIPS creates problems for countries wanting access to pharmaceuticals. The UNDP has drawn attention to the implications of TRIPS to technology transfer and human development (UNDP 2001). The nature and extent of conflicts between aims of WTO agreements and other international agreements has been debated in relation to human rights committments and e.g. the Biodiversity Convention and Biosafety Protocol (United Nations 2001ab, Final Report 2000, Phillips and Kerr 2000). Finally, various UN summits and conferences have tackled matters arising from the intersection of trade and health.

While trade policies should recognise social concerns, such policies – and trade experts – may not be the best forums to decide these matters. In other words, decisions about non-trade issues should be made in non-trade forums. There seems to be more willingness on the part of the developing countries to shift these matters of substance to UN agencies rather than to include them directly as part of the trade agenda. This enhances the support for the broader UN system to become more engaged in matters dealing with health, environment, labour and culture to ensure that trade interests do not override other policy priorities.

The problem with substance matters is that there seems to be a tendency to shift them away from the UN bodies rather than to them and deal with them through more liberalisation and property rights friendly organisations such as the OECD, the World Bank, the World Intellectual Property Organisation (WIPO) or ad hoc bodies. Braithwaithe and Drahos have called this as "forum shifting", where politically problematic matter are shifted to forums where these can be run through better (Braithwaithe and Drahos 1999). In relation to health policies, there seems to be a general risk of forum shifting *away* from the WHO and other UN organisations towards the international financial institutions, such as the World Bank, and OECD or ad hoc organisations, industry led bodies or specific meetings. This is of concern especially when standard setting functions are of importance as corporate bodies, moreover, would prefer their practices to be governed by voluntary codes (rather than legally binding measures). But it is unlikely that ad hoc voluntary measures will deliver sustainable improvements in area in which where the corporate sector has a direct interest and in which the measures might dent profits. There is also a risk that substantial decision-making power will move to publicly-unaccountable bodies representing particular corporate interests.

Overall, there is a general gap in decision-making across the globe on health matters in comparison to trade matters. But while there are certain disagreements between countries, from a strictly health point of view and when considering the medium- and long-term, there are common and shared interests in health across countries (*see e.g.* Koivusalo 1999). Some common aspects are already recognised, for instance, the health implications of trade in substances that are hazardous to health and infectious diseases and epidemics. Nonetheless, health issues are mostly dealt with in a national, if not local, context. This easily creates a gap in decision-making which then worsens at global level. The lack of substance debates also results in policy choices, which may favour exporters or rights holders of particular countries, at the cost of their health policies and citizens. The current trend on emphasising the role of NGOs and civil society consultations has also complicated some public interests in health systems as NGOs often articulate in a very charity oriented and residual framework of public policies or see single issue or disease campaigning as more effective than broader policy work.

3. The impact of WTO trade agreements on health

3.1 Food security, nutrition and consumption of hazardous foods

In the forthcoming renegotiations of the WTO Agreements, as agreed at the 2001 Doha Ministerial, many developing countries are likely to focus their attention on the Agreement on Agriculture. A better regulatory system in the global trade of agricultural products may well enhance the economic prospects of the developing world. But it is uncertain to what extent more liberalised markets in agriculture would enhance food security within these countries. Trade proponents often strive to separate food security from food production – in other words, to divide a country's capacity to buy food from its capacity to cultivate food crops for domestic consumption. However, liberalisation of trade in agriculture has also been criticised because poorer sections of society may subsequently find themselves unable to buy foodstuffs if domestic prices increase as a result of increased production for export or of shifting cultivation towards more lucrative export markets. Any problems in food security or in the prices of basic commodities may have the strongest impacts not only on the poorest countries, but also on the poorest people within richer countries. Although such countries which may seem to be the main beneficiaries of reaping profits from agricultural exports, these profits may come at the cost of higher domestic prices or of more volatile markets in and prices of essential products.

In food and agricultural trade, the net trade position of the developing countries as a whole has worsened between 1990–1994 and 1995–1999 due to sharp increases in food imports and despite marked increases in agricultural exports (Sharma 2002). Actors such as the US-based, Food First Institute, have highlighted the limits of the benefits of increased 'market access'. It argues that the easing of tariff restrictions in developing countries in the current economic climate would be suicidal as long as the developed world maintains its agricultural subsidies. Furthermore, as most countries export only about 10% of the value of their food production, keeping 90% for their home market, there is a danger that, in the hope of increasing their 10% share, developing countries will actually yield some of their 90% share to imports from the US and the EU (Food First 2002). The developmental impact of the agricultural subsidies paid by developed countries to their farmers and of food dumping on international markets have been criticised heavily not only by the developing world, but also by several non-governmental organisations (Action Aid 2002, OXFAM 2002a-c). The World Bank chief economist has lately joint to the critics of agricultural subsidies and, interestingly, used growing of sugar beet in Finland as a prime example of this folly (Stern 2002).

In terms of health, some agricultural subsidies are worse than others. European Community subsidies to tobacco farming in European Community practically subsidises exports as the low quality doe not allow its sale on European markets. Tobacco exports and subsidies are particularly hard to justify from a health perspective. European Community priorities are clear, however: European Community spending on public health is comparable to 5% of the subsidies granted to tobacco farming (Eisma 1999).

Agricultural production relates to basic consumption and subsistence. The expansion of production for export may carry further risks for countries, especially if many countries embark on a similar course, leading to lower prices overall. The prices of primary commodities also tend to fluctuate more than those of manufactured commodities. Further liberalisation of trade in agricultural products may also lead to some countries dumping their surplus produce on global markets and thereby squeezing out local production in unsustainable ways.

The further global integration of food and agricultural markets is usually assumed to lead to better nutrition, however, it may also lead to a deterioration in people's diets if local food production is replaced by a less nutritious alternative source from global markets. Countries should be able to ensure that they can maintain variation in crop structure and production at national and local levels if they so wish. As produce destined for export are often cultivated on larger unit sizes, it would be important to ensure that any benefits gained from increased exports do not accrue to larger farms and estates only, but benefit a broad range of farmers. It would also be important to ensure that mechanisms are in place to support also small farmers in a more liberalised environment. While the current regime of agricultural subsidies serves to increase the gap between small-scale and large farmers, countries should take care not to opt for a solution that only increases it still further, if, as may be expected, the larger producers are more able to take advantage of a more liberalised environment.

A substantial part of global markets trade in products of questionable or detrimental effects on health – tobacco, alcohol and soft drinks are just a few examples. In addition, sometimes the products are not a problem, but their cost and way of using. This is the case of infant feeding supplements and breastmilk substitutes in developing countries. The implementation of the WHO's code governing the marketing of breast-milk substitutes has been construed to tackle the problematic impact of marketing of breast-milk substitutes on infant feeding practices (WHO 1981). Trade-related arguments have already been used to counter the legitimate activities of countries in implementing the WHO Code. In the so-called Gerber case, for instance, Gerber claimed in that it should be allowed to use its baby-picture, prohibited by the Guatemalan authorities as contravening the Code, because it was part of Gerber's trade-mark (*see* e.g. Koivusalo 2001; Mokhiber 1996).

Trade liberalisation has been important for the trade of tobacco and tobacco products. The GATT Uruguay Round facilitated penetration of the world's tobacco markets by the transnational tobacco companies and, for the first time, included agreements to liberalise trade in unmanufactured tobacco. China, Eastern Europe and African countries have been seen as particularly attractive new markets for the tobacco industry as well as targeting women and young persons (Bettcher et al 2000). Tobacco company Philip Morris admits to having a large stake in market access negotiations. As foreign barriers to imports are lowered, the company stands to boost exports significantly. (Bettcher et al 2000) The paradox of tobacco trade is that, taking into account health and other costs, every 1000 additional tonnes of tobacco traded in the global markets results in a net loss of US$ 27.2 million (Barnum 1994).

While tobacco is amongst the most important health hazardous products, it is not the only product. Alcohol has so far claimed limited attention in the international agenda, yet in many ways international markets and brands are becoming more important also in the developing world. Trade in alcohol has also been promoted by major trade actors, such as the European Community, which has been active in advancing the interests of the European alcohol industry in foreign markets (*see* e.g. WTO 1996).

3.1.1 Health policy issues

From a country's health policy perspective, it is crucially important to ensure sufficient availability of nutritious food for the whole population and to ensure that food security is not compromised. Certain national concerns about food security and crop structure need to be accommodated in any negotiations on further international trade in agriculture. The role of domestic agricultural production in people's daily survival is greater in developing countries than in the developed world. Thus any mismanagement of the global trade in agricultural products would be felt more strongly in developing countries, which should, therefore, be allowed to maintain and implement more safeguards.

The transport of food products can also cause problems, especially of foods which carry a high risk of becoming contaminated, such as fresh or frozen milk, meat, fish and seafood products. Mechanisms to favour local food production should not be automatically regarded as protectionist. The ability of a country to ensure its food security at a national level must be respected during the negotiation process and needs to be seen in the development context as developing countries will have less operational space to replace losses if prices of crops decrease or fluctuate a lot.

There are few, if any, health grounds for supporting subsidies for tobacco cultivation or for exporting tobacco products. Another agricultural product of lesser nutritious value is sugar, which is hardly a basic staple requiring the current level of subsidies it enjoys in the developed world.

The prices of products do influence consumption patterns and can be an important mechanism to guide consumption towards healthier products. Countries should therefore maintain the option of being able to use price mechanisms in order to influence consumption even if they liberalise agriculture.

More liberal markets can lead to more trade in substances which have detrimental effects on people's health in short and long term. Increased consumption of tobacco, alcohol, soft-drinks, candies, fat, meat, processed foods and the inappropriate use of breast-milk substitutes would be reflected in people's health status. Globalisation and liberalisation may lead to economic growth, but from a health policy perspective, consumption that may be good for economics is not necessarily good for health.

These are not matters of marginal relevance. Tobacco control is one of the most rational evidence-based policies in medicine. Estimates indicate that tobacco use was responsible for 3 million deaths in 1990 and reached 4 million in 1998 and is expected to reach 8.4 million by 2020, of which 70% will occur in developing countries. Penetration of new markets by aggressive multinational companies is one of the factors that has prevented the public health community from effectively implementing tobacco control policies. Recent empirical findings support the expectations of increasing domestic consumption as a result of increased trade and suggest that less wealthy countries may be more vulnerable than wealthier countries to the impact of trade liberalisation on cigarette consumption (Bettcher et al 2000).

It is generally claimed by advocates of increased trade liberalisation that the trade rules do not prohibit countries from regulating. But the practical implementation of this claim is to prefer the least trade restrictive mechanism. This affects public health regulations. Personal or individual health education and promotion, for instance, would be regarded as the least market restrictive mechanism, while any measures related to pricing, advertising, distribution or access would probably be interpreted as more trade restrictive. Banning the advertising of certain products, meanwhile, would particularly affect those products aiming for new markets and thus could be interpreted as a subsidy to domestic producers. Policy measures related to pricing or distribution of products may also generate claims of differential treatment. The negotiation of the Framework Convention on Tobacco Control (FCTC) in the WHO has unfolded against a background of awareness of health and other human rights. The negotiations will also test the strength of the international community to tackle matters where substantial economic interests are involved as it is likely that there will be overlap and potential conflict between FCTC and WTO obligations. It is also known that tobacco companies are prepared and willing to use trade agreements related arguments to dismantle both national efforts to curb smoking through legislation on marketing and imposing warnings on packages as well as in influencing the process of FCTC negotiations.

In the developing world, public health regulatory measures relating to tobacco, alcohol and breast-milk substitutes will be of particular importance. The WHO Code on the marketing of breast-milk substitutes and infant foods should provide some support to countries. However, it is clear that especially in countries such as China vast prospects for expanding markets can be seen as parents are willing and able to invest on their only or few children more. The marketing of breast-milk substitutes is only one example of the problematic aspects of products with less clear product-related health implications, but which can be still of major importance. The use of antibiotics in cattle raising, cultivation and fish farming can be raised as one issue. The efforts to guide consumption towards less and healthier fat consumption or to limit the use of sugary products and fast foods applies also to many developing countries.

It is unlikely that any government will appeal on matters related to tobacco, but it is clear that problematic appeals to dispute settlement have been made, one example being that of asbestos regulations, which luckily ended in a decision favoring more the public health viewpoints (WTO 1998; WTO 2001a). Whether or not a dispute settlement case will emerge is one issue, the more informal lobbying and pressure towards weaker governments may well lead to dismantling of public health regulations on the basis of claims and threats of trade restrictiveness. It is thus critical to ensure that developing country governments are not bullied by industries citing trade-related arguments into abandoning their public health regulations that aim to limit the consumption of products that have problematic health consequences.

Finally, one current and future broader policy concern is that development issues are relegated to being merely another aspect of the broader trade interests of the developed world. In the area of agriculture and food one of the issues where this is likely is related to the labeling requirements of GMO products as well as their treatment in the context of trade in agriculture.

3.1.2 Policy advice from health perspective

1) The main policy challenge from health perspective is to ensure that food security in developing countries and nutritional value of available food for the whole population is not compromised as liberalization efforts proceed.

2) The increasing transport of food products longer distances is problematic especially with respect of substances with high risk of contamination. It would be meaningful to ensure that mechanisms, which favor local production, would not be treated automatically as means of protectionism and that scope to ensure food security at national level is respected during the negotiation process.

3) On behalf of the European Community one challenge is to ensure that negotiations do not focus on how public health regulations restrict agricultural trade as a way to divert attention from export subsidies. In agricultural trade some products are more health promoting than others. There is no health reason to support subsidies to cultivation or export of health hazardous products, such as tobacco. Countries should also have possibilities to use price mechanisms to guide consumption of products, such as sugar.

4) The role of agricultural production to daily survival of populations is larger in the developing countries, which should be allowed more safeguards and flexibilities in the area.

5) Globalization and more liberalized markets in goods deal also with substances of problematic health value. It is necessary to recognize the need for regulatory public health policies on the basis of health concerns and especially with respect to limiting consumption of products hazardous to health, such as tobacco or alcohol, or guiding of consumption of products which are costly, second best or problematic when used inappropriately, such as infant foods and breastmilk substitutes. While globalization and liberalization may lead to economic growth, the health policy concern is that all consumption, which may be good for economics, is not good for health. Developing countries should have space to have broad public health policies without threat of a trade dispute.

6) It is likely that the role and prospects of GMO products will also be debated in the context of trade in agriculture and labeling. In this it is necessary to ensure that developmental arguments are not misused merely to ensure free markets for GMO products.

7) It is important to recognise that livelihoods and local production capacities are not crushed in both developing and developed countries. However, it is of more essential

importance in the developing world where agriculture is mostly not a commercial operation, but carried out largely on small and household farms.

3.2 The Agreement on Trade-Related Aspects of Intellectual Property Rights (TRIPS)

The WTO's Agreement on Trade-Related Aspects of Intellectual Property Rights or TRIPS has gained growing criticism with respect to access to pharmaceuticals from developing countries, but this criticism is only a tip of the iceberg of a much broader debate on balance of the agreement between interests of right holders and users and its relevance to technology transfer. UNDP Human Development Report 2001 highlighted concerns related to technological change and concerns over data access and availability became evident in the European Community commissioned report on TRIPS and Biodiversity issues (UNDP 2001; Final Report 2000). The most recent and perhaps most comprehensive contribution to this debate has been the United Kingdom commissioned analysis by the Committee on Intellectual Property Rights (CIPR), which published their report in September 2002. The CIPR focussed specifically on development aspects and has brought critical views on TRIPS into more mainstream trade and development forums (CIPR 2002).

The role of industry in negotiating and promoting the TRIPS Agreement is known (see e.g. Drahos 1995; Drahos 1997), but the implications of the Agreement have generally been debated in the contexts of the varying interests of different countries; less explored have been the different implications for the public and for the corporate sectors, or the contrasting implications for consumers and the right holders of intellectual property rights.

In terms of health, the TRIPS agreement is primarily relevant to the research, development, pricing and licensing of pharmaceuticals and other health technologies. The broader public debate on TRIPS and access to pharmaceuticals started when WHO published a booklet *'Globalisation and access to pharmaceuticals'* and the World Health Assembly proposed resolution on the matter (Velasquez and Boulet 1997, WHO 1998a). After a heated debate and extensive lobbying, the World Health Assembly passed a resolution in 1998 with minor changes and the WHO published a revised version of its book on TRIPS correcting technical errors. One of the major concerns in the original resolution was the emphasis on primacy of public health in comparison to commercial rights, which was initially opposed by the United States and the European Commission. The European member states were confronted with a then Committee 113 resolution that health and commercial rights should not be contrasted. Since the adoption of the WHA resolution, TRIPS and access to pharmaceuticals have been on the agenda of most UN meetings. Pharmaceutical industry and countries supporting the interests of the rights holders – in practice the pharmaceutical industry – have often attempted to narrow the interpretation of the specific stipulations in the agreement on compulsory licensing and rights to use compulsory licensing. The stands of the European Commission have been consistently restrictive and systematically supportive of narrow interpretations of the rights of countries to use compulsory licensing. The use of compulsory licensing was considered to be legitimate only in grave public health crisis, although this limitation in practice relates merely to the use of compulsory licensing without consulting the rights holder and not using of compulsory licensing as such.

Finally, the Doha Ministerial Conference in 2001 addressed the matter in a declaration and asked the TRIPS Council to look into the issue of exports of pharmaceuticals produced under compulsory licence. Without this option, many smaller and poorer countries would not be able to use effectively the compulsory licensing clause to gain access to patented pharmaceuticals, as they do not have the capacity to manufacture themselves (paragraph 6 negotiations). WHO has since published a book on the implications of the Doha declaration on the TRIPS agreement and public health (Correa 2002a, annex 1). In some ways the Doha declaration cleared air on the question of primacy of public health concerns, but debate on compulsory licensing has continued in the TRIPS Council in relation to so called paragraph 6 negotiations and in December 2002 was still unresolved. The initial views towards consensus may have been influenced also by the attempts of the US and Canada to issue compulsory licenses in the aftermath of September 11 and when anthrax scares were at highest (see e.g. Abbot 2002). The initial interest in settling the matter seems to have diminished and the old divisions between narrower and broader interpretations of TRIPS resurfaced the debates again in December 2002.

3.2.1 Health policy issues

Debates about health and access to pharmaceuticals have focused on the least developed countries. The mechanisms proposed to alleviate the problem have often been limited to the least developed countries only. But in terms of health and access to pharmaceuticals, the least developed countries tend to be less able to benefit from many newer more sophisticated treatments which are those under patent and protected through TRIPS, for instance, HIV/AIDS treatment. Such countries would often get more value for what money they do have if they spent it on prevention, including specific measures such as preventing mother-to-child transmission. The least developed countries lack many resources, including access to most pharmaceuticals, even essential drugs that have usually run out of the patent protection. From the perspective of health policies, restricting support for gaining access to patented pharmaceuticals to the least developed countries does not make sense in terms of capacity to benefit.

Moreover, these are often the countries which do not have to implement the TRIPS agreement yet or in which pharmaceutical companies do not even seek patent protection.

This being said it is important to note that, while the TRIPS agreement might not be the top of the agenda of the least developing countries, this does not mean that it is irrelevant to them. In spite of the rights of not to implement the treaty yet, TRIPS or even its broader versions has been included in bilateral treaties. The problem of bilateral treaties has been brought up recently (OXFAM 2002d, Drahos 2001). It is also the poorest countries that often pay the largest share of their meagre budgets on pharmaceuticals. Health care costs in general can be crudely divided into personnel, infrastructure and technology costs. In poorer countries, personnel costs are generally lower than in richer countries. WHO estimates show that the share of pharmaceutical costs in the overall health budget of developing countries can be as high as 60% (WHO 1998b). For many smaller and poorer countries, the availability of cheaper pharmaceuticals is directly related to their access to generic pharmaceuticals (those no longer protected by patents) manufactured in larger countries for more competitive markets. As price of pharmaceuticals may drop to only a fraction of its price when patented, the swift access to generic pharmaceuticals is in the interest of health policies and cannot be reduced to disputes between industries. The access to pharmaceuticals is also affected in many countries by policies of major producers of generic pharmaceuticals.

It is of importance to consider health policies beyond pharmaceuticals as otherwise there is danger of over emphasis on pharmaceutical solutions. In many countries, both rich and poor, large public spending and focus on pharmaceutical procurement is not always wise, cost-effective or medically sound, creating dangers of inappropriate care and an increase in drug resistance from disease-causing microbes. The HIV/AIDS crisis has dominated debates on TRIPS and access to pharmaceuticals and has on its part led to huge expectations of governments, some of whom have been reluctant to commit themselves to providing costly and continuous treatment for substantial numbers of their populations. This is further aggravated by the fact that HIV/AIDS drugs do not cure the disease and need to be provided for the lifetime of an infected person to delay the onset of AIDS itself. In many countries, even if patients were to receive the medicines for free, it would be difficult to ensure that adequate treatment and care were available to all those in need simply because of the limits in human resources.

The major beneficiaries of cheaper patented pharmaceuticals, particularly treatments for HIV/AIDS, would be those infected in the middle-income countries such as Brazil, Thailand and South Africa, which would otherwise spend disproportionate amounts of their health budgets dealing with just one disease. Brazil has shown that public health programmes do matter in terms of HIV/AIDS and that compulsory licensing –

or at least the threat of it – can lower prices. The prices of key pharmaceuticals decreased quickly as result of Brasilias stepped towards the use of compulsory licensing.

From a health policy perspective, the emphasis and limitation of TRIPS related measures to least developed countries is not meaningful. It is also clear that while in many least developed countries TRIPS is not an immediate concern, it does bear substantial relevance indirectly. The most sustainable way of ensuring access to pharmaceuticals in poorer developing countries is using and prioritising essential pharmaceuticals; producing or importing generic pharmaceuticals; and when necessary compulsory licensing of patented pharmaceuticals. Most UN agencies working with health recognise this.

There are no free markets of pharmaceuticals. In practice at least half of pharmaceuticals are paid by public resources. The rest is financed by those ill. Higher pharmaceutical costs tend to be reflected in higher overall health care costs everywhere in the world. In many developing countries the costs of health care and ill health are a major cause of people falling into poverty. The costs of pharmaceuticals are rising everywhere. Some HIV/AIDS medications can certainly be used effectively in poor countries, but they cannot be regarded as any "over-the-counter" pharmaceutical if they are to remain safe and effective. An overemphasis on access to pharmaceuticals can further disrupt health policies in many developing countries and shift resources from other areas through the inappropriate use and sale of pharmaceuticals.

In terms of price, the issues about access to pharmaceuticals in developing countries are just the tip of the iceberg: the major implications of pricing are in the *developed* world. Many recent documents have stressed this in their discussions about public goods and the responsibilities of the developed world. Ultimately, debates about TRIPS and pharmaceutical pricing are not only about access to pharmaceuticals in the developing world: but about fairness and greed. This is why focus on access questions seems to be used also to obscure the growing concern over the growing costs of pharmaceuticals and exorbitant prices of drugs.

Patenting and pricing

The actual production costs of pharmaceuticals are usually a fraction of what they are sold for. The higher prices of patented pharmaceuticals are considered as the reward for research and development efforts. TRIPS allows the rights-holder to have a monopoly over their product for 20 years both as a reward for investment into research and development and as an incentive for further investment. In practice, this leads to monopoly pricing and higher costs of pharmaceuticals. The costs of pharmaceuticals in any given country are related to the structure and scope of the markets. But there is little doubt that the growing costs of new technologies are due to stronger intellectual property right protection, which prevent competition from bringing down the costs of a particular pharmaceutical. But patents are of value only if there is relevant competition. In many poorer countries, pharmaceuticals are not patented simply because there is no competition in the area. This is the case in many African countries (*see* e.g. CIPR 2002). In some cases the problem can be the lack of incentives to produce medicines due to low profit margins.

One of the means to tackle monopoly pricing is compulsory licensing and it – or the threat of it – remains an important part of the legitimate rights of governments to interfere on the basis of various reasons, including those of public health. As Ministries of Health would be those using the option of compulsory licensing, it is in their interest to ensure that the procedure would be as broadly available and as easy to implement as possible. In any given country, it is the Ministry of Health that needs to tackle the high costs of pharmaceuticals. It is thus in the interests of health policy to support the use of compulsory licensing, whereas it is in the interest of the rights' holders to support as narrow interpretation of this right as possible. This conflict of interests has continued even after the Doha Declaration on the TRIPS Agreement and public health (WTO 2001b). For many smaller countries, compulsory licensing is irrelevant or meaningless unless they are allowed to import on the basis of compulsory licensing. The European Commission and the US have lobbied for a narrow measure limited mostly to least developed countries and HIV/AIDS, malaria and tuberculosis. The US has later changed the scope of diseases to cover infectious diseases, however, there is no health reason for this limitation and all health arguments would favour a stand of not limiting the scope of diseases.

The developing world, which have gained support from the European Parliament (European Parliament 2002), have promoted broader rights for exports on the basis of compulsory licensing. The restriction of compulsory licensing to certain diseases results in a "disease apartheid" whereby patients suffering from some diseases are in a better position than those others suffering more others. When diseases that affect smaller numbers of people are considered, the option to import becomes even more significant. The higher costs of pharmaceuticals for these smaller disease groups could well be borne by some countries' governments. But it is difficult to argue why treating of a small disease group should gain a disproportionally large share of the total pharmaceutical budget. An example used with respect to this problem has been the relatively high costs of the new drugs for Multiple Sclerosis (MS). From a health perspective, there is no reason to restrict countries which can use compulsory licensing mechanisms to import pharmaceuticals or to act as producers for export. Moreover, health needs for compulsory licensing may emerge in developed countries with smaller markets as competitive pricing and viable production can often be achieved only for larger markets. In many ways, the current proposed restrictions on compulsory licensing are not driven by health concerns. They are driven by the interests of rights holders (in this case primarily the multinational pharmaceutical industry) and advocated by governments acting on their behalf – and health concerns and public interests are being compromised.

It can be argued that in the context of manufacturing capacity one crucial aspect of access to pharmaceuticals is price. The simplest and often most meaningful way of defining a problems in manufacturing capacity is to use the price of the pharmaceutical as a reference. If a country cannot produce a patented pharmaceutical locally at lower costs through using compulsory licensing, it should be able to import the pharmaceutical from another country which can. It could be argued that this country lacks the manufacturing capacity to provide the drug on a sufficiently low price.

Even though the TRIPS Agreement does not prohibit parallel imports, the topic has frequently been included in TRIPS debates. These debates have often implied that TRIPS would prohibit parallel imports, however, in countries where patent laws apply international exhaustion of rights, parallel imports are TRIPS compatible (see e.g. Correa 2002a, WTO/WHO 2001). The rights to use international exhaustion of rights was also referred to in the Doha declaration sub-paragraph 5, stating that 'is to leave each member free to establish its own regime for such exhaustion without challenge' (see e.g. Doha declaration 2001; Correa 2002a). European Community has paid especially attention to the use of tiered pricing – i.e. offering pharmaceuticals cheaper for poorer populations – than to parallel imports. While tiered pricing implicitly assumes a segmented market overall, parallel importing can be a mechanism to diminish pharmaceutical price differences between countries. However, while TRIPS does not prohibit countries to use measures to counter parallel imports e.g. in the developed countries, it is clear that tiered pricing cannot be used to prohibit or pressure developing countries not to use parallel importing. The same applies to the rights of using compulsory licensing. While there is nothing amiss with pharmaceutical corporations using tiered pricing, it is necessary to ensure that public funds and resources are not misallocated in supporting tiered-priced products when the same products could be obtained more cost-effectively through compulsory licensing or from generic producers.

Research and development efforts in health technologies

The assumptions underlying the TRIPs agreement are that patents ensure that innovations eventually become publicly available (the patent holder must publish details of their invention) and that investments are directed towards important areas. But the current focus of investment in the research and development of pharmaceuticals clearly indicates the problems with this approach.

The IPR Commission pointed out that, in the corporate sector, research and development costs is predominantly geared to larger markets and to the diseases of more affluent populations. These account for about 95% of investments, and just 5% goes toward diseases of major importance to developing countries (CIPR 2002). Furthermore, while the emphasis is on incentives to R&D these may not automatically lead to production of pharmaceuticals. Take, for example, sleeping sickness. The drug, eflornithine, which can treat it was not profitable enough to warrant production. It became easily accessible, however, when it was used in a new hair-removing drug – and was then donated free by the industry (McNeil 2001). The same problem of market-driven research applies also to the developed world. Research and development is not be driven by health problems and needs, but by prospective and profitable markets.

Recognition of the problems in investment on R&D and especially those for developing country diseases has led to initiatives of providing aid, incentives and funds aimed at attracting the interest of the private sector in high priority diseases of the poor. The European Commission's programme on poverty reduction aims to channel funds to clinical trials in developing countries and pharmaceutical research (European Commission 2001a). It is clear that public money will be needed in the area of research on diseases affecting mostly developing world, however, the danger in the current processes is that if the corporate sector and their affiliates become the recipients of the funds without attention to intellectual property rights, the costs covered by aid money to carry out clinical trials and research are the very costs that the protection of intellectual property rights were meant to recoup. This additional funding simply pays the corporate sector for their research and development efforts again, and is, in effect, a public subsidy to corporations. Substantial amounts of public funds will need to be invested in pharmaceutical research, both at global and national levels, if medical and public health priorities are to be met. However, it is important that these funds are used in a way which supports these aims most effectively. In the context of intellectual property rights it is also important that intellectual property rights granted to the products of publicly-funded research support public access to knowledge and support technology transfer and that benefits accrue to the public, rather than the corporate, sector.

The recent emphasis on pharmaceutical research and development as a global public good and the consequent necessity for the developed world to pay higher prices as a trade-off for creating access to pharmaceuticals in the developing world is problematic. Firstly, it gives the incorrect impression that higher pharmaceutical costs in the developed world have to be accepted mostly in order to ensure access to pharmaceuticals to developing countries. Secondly, it creates little incentive to ensure that health-related priorities are reflected in the future R&D efforts within the corporate sector. Developed countries will certainly need to pay more in order to ensure that R&D is carried out on diseases prevalent in the developing world. But the ethical requirement to solidarity with respect to developing countries does not specify how this should be done and the mere acceptance of higher costs of pharmaceuticals due to plight of the developing world may in the end act merely as a smokescreen to obscure the more mundane causes – such as profiteering or inefficiencies – for the rising costs or overpricing of pharmaceuticals in the developed world, while doing little or nothing to address the real and legitimate concerns of the developing world.

In terms of health and development policies, protection of intellectual property rights may not be an effective means of enhancing R&D. Moreover, it may do more to limit rather than increase exchange of information. For diagnostic tests, there is no need to carry out long clinical trials, so the 20-year patent may be unwarranted. The Commission on Intellectual Property Rights drew attention to various aspects of TRIPS which have not been debated previously in the context of the TRIPS Agreement and has put forward as well as suggested mechanisms for patent reforms in developing countries (see Annex 2).

The pharmaceutical industry has given estimates of its research and development costs, but the actual structure of pharmaceutical costs is not known. There is some evidence that advertising costs and returns to shareholders have grown faster pace than research and development costs (Tarabusi and Vickery 1997). There have also been few new innovations: the majority of new drugs are in fact so-called "me-too" drugs, which closely resemble of those already on the market.

Pharmaceutical licensing

National authorities usually require registrants of pharmaceutical products to submit data on the physical and chemical composition of a product, as well as information on its quality, safety and efficacy (so-called "test data"). TRIPS Article 39.3 requires governments to provide protection for this marketing approval data.

Disagreement has arisen over the interpretation of this article. The pharmaceutical industry and some countries have argued for a broad coverage of Article 39.3 and for a requirement that countries grant exclusive rights to the originators of marketing approval data. But during the TRIPS negotiations, negotiators specifically considered and rejected language granting of exclusive rights to test data. They stated that Article 39.3. should be interpreted narrowly and that it should not allow protection of already-public data but only for new chemical entities. Prior to granting protection, the Article allows national regulatory authorities to request the applicant to prove that the information for which protection is sought is the result of significant investment. It has been further argued that countries have considerable discretion to define "unfair" in the context of their own laws and culture. It has also been argued that countries can meet their obligations to protect against "unfair" commercial use under Article 39.3 by barring "dishonest" uses of test data. Moreover, countries are not obligated under

Article 39.3. to confer exclusive rights on the originator of the marketing approval data (Correa 2002b).

The interpretation of Article 39.3 has become a battleground between producers of generic pharmaceuticals (those that are off patent) and the research-based pharmaceutical industry. A narrow interpretation would force the generic industry to provide new studies on test data and bio-availability if it wanted to register a drug for licensed use, rather than use existing studies. This would hamper the abilities of the generic industry to gain access to markets and would increase their costs. While this interpretation would benefit the research-based pharmaceutical industry, its overall effectiveness is questionable in cases where the product – and therefore the test data – would effectively be the same.

In terms of health policies, access to affordable pharmaceuticals is important. But there are other health policy-focused reasons to support a narrow interpretation of Article 39.3. A broad interpretation of the commitment to data disclosure against unfair commercial use is problematic: any research or analysis that might be regarded as against the interests of the pharmaceutical industry may be interpreted as "unfair commercial use". Even access to published studies have been curtailed on the basis of commercial arguments such as commercial confidentiality or secrecy. The danger is that public accountability of government procedures, transparency and the potential to ensure that possible adverse effects of pharmaceuticals are adequately dealt with may be compromised. From a health point of view, openness after a registration decision has been made would benefit citizens and consumers more than non-disclosure on a broadly-defined basis.

Trademarks and health education

The Agreement on Trade-Related Aspects of Intellectual Property Rights provides protection not only for patents but also for trademarks. Because many governments have been either introducing warnings or scaring pictures on tobacco packages or insisting that companies remove the word "light" from the name of cigarettes, the tobacco industry has used the stipulations on protection of trademarks under TRIPS to limit such activities (Philip Morris 2001). Trademark issues may be raised in the future also in the context of the international code on the marketing of breast-milk substitutes and infant foods. Gerber, for instance, claimed that its baby-picture in advertisements was part of its trademark (*see* "food security" section earlier) (Koivusalo 2001; Mokhiber 1997).

From a health policy perspective, it is important to ensure that relatively weaker Southern governments are supported in their efforts to curb smoking and alcohol use or to promote breast-feeding as part of their public health policies and that other countries or companies do not use TRIPS inappropriately to limit legitimate public health policies.

Article 27(b), indigenous knowledge, agriculture and copyrights

TRIPS Article 27(b) deals with what can and cannot be patented. Patentability has become an issue connected to biodiversity while the patentability of animals and plants, including genes and genetically-modified plants and animals has generated substantial controversy. The recent analysis of the UK's Commission on Intellectual Property Rights expressed reservations about the possible impact of patents on plants and animals in general. In the absence of any universally-recognised definition of what constitutes a micro-organism, it suggests that developing countries should remain free to adopt their own credible definition that limits the range of material covered (CIPR 2002) The patentability of living organisms and genes also touches on broader ethical and technical concerns, such as the extent of innovation and the restrictive impact of patents on research and development.

In the field of agriculture, certain innovations such as "golden rice", a rice genetically engineered to have higher vitamin A content, have been portrayed as one solution to better nutrition and health in the developing world. The 2001 UNDP Human Development Report on technology transfer argued that the capacities of developing countries to benefit from agricultural and biotechnological innovations was of crucial importance (UNDP 2001). The CIPR report meanwhile stressed the importance of research in the public domain in contrast to the usual emphasis on GM aspects. Just as the so-called Green Revolution – high yielding crops requiring large inputs of water and chemicals – which was developed and applied with the public sector, failed to reach poorer farmers, so it is apparent that research into genetically engineered crops which is led by the private sector will be even less likely to do so. (CIPR 2002)

While there are health concerns related to GM products, the most important in the developing world context is the possibility of expansion of seeds engineered with termination of germination has raised special concern in the developing world, where farmers still collect seeds to cultivate next year. Critics and NGOs have consistently highlighted the problems of divergent interests of subsistence farmers and the expanding seeds industry. They have stressed the dangers of commercialisation and multinationalisation of seeds and agricultural technology and research at the expense of poorer farmers and their interests (see e.g. Shiva 2001).

Some questions about bio-piracy and indigenous knowledge that have emerged in the context of TRIPS also relate to health and health-related products. Vandana Shiva has defined piracy at three levels (Shiva 2001).

1) Resource piracy in which the biological and natural resources of communities and the country are freely taken, without recognition of permission, and are used to build up global economies.

2) Intellectual and cultural piracy in which the cultural and intellectual heritage of communities and the country is freely taken without recognition or permission and is used for claiming IPRs such as patents and trademark, even though the primary innovation and creativity, has not taken place through corporate investment,

3) Economic piracy in which domestic and international markets are usurped through the use of trade names and IPRs, thereby distroying local economies and national economies where the original innovation took place and hence wiping out the livelihoods and economic survival of millions.

Two substances, turmeric and neem, for which the patents were subsequently revoked were patented on the basis of their health-related impacts. These cases reflect the major concern connected to biopiracy and indigenous knowledge is that patents may be granted for "inventions" which are not really novel or inventive at all once traditional knowledge already in the public domain is taken into account.

Implementation

Implementing TRIPS may well impose relatively large costs on smaller and poorer countries that could spend their public resources more efficiently on education and health, for example. The CIPR considered several implementing possibilities, which offer prospects for developing countries to tailor intellectual property rights to their particular developmental aims and capacities (CIPR 2002).

Many of the poorest countries do not have to implement the agreement yet. But it is likely that other countries that are major producers of generic pharmaceuticals, such as India, will already be affected by TRIPS compliance, even though they are not yet obliged to comply with the Agreement. This means that TRIPS cannot be set aside simply because the least developed countries do not have to comply with it for another decade or more. Another issue is the TRIPS compliance required in bilateral treaties, which basically eats up the given leverage in implementation in many cases (see e.g. CIPR 2002).

Future concerns

Controversial as TRIPS already is, it is probable that not all TRIPS and development-related matters have surfaced yet. In terms of future policies, it is important to recognise that both the developed and developing world face similar problems in terms of health policies. TRIPS is likely to increase the emphasis on innovation and patenting in many developing countries. But it is unlikely that this capacity for innovation in the pharmaceutical sector will be primarily directed either towards addressing the diseases of the poor or towards public health priorities in a broader sense.

It is thus important to ensure that debates about TRIPS and its implications for overall human development are not reduced to issues between developing and developed countries only: they must also consider crucial substance matters (such as health and the environment); cultural and socio-economic impacts and rights (for instance, relating to indigenous populations and traditional knowledge, and the tension between public and private interests); the impacts at a national level (public interests and costs versus the (corporate) rights-holders' interests and costs); and the impacts on research and innovation (access to knowledge, focus of research).

In the future, it is probable that a range of further problems will climb up the agenda: those encountered among the research and development community because of patenting; access to information; the ethics of patent protection and patentability; technology transfer in biotechnologies and information technologies; benefit sharing; and indigenous and cultural rights. It is also likely that criticisms from the developing world about how TRIPS closes off several development options to them will increase. Such demands are unlikely to be satisfied with limited exceptions on access to pharmaceuticals to treat a few specified diseases only.

Overall, there seems to be a wider consensus that TRIPS is unlikely to enhance growth or increase social equality in developing countries, which was only recently brought to the more mainstream debates (CIPR 2002). In its present formulation, a large share of the benefits will accrue to developed countries, particularly to their corporate sectors. While the rights holders in developed countries may be regarded as the winners on the whole, this does not mean that the developed country governments are necessarily winners with respect to many aspects of the TRIPS Agreement. It is thus necessary to pay attention to the costs and benefits in the field of health and other fields, such as education. If the public sector and the most vulnerable sectors of society are predominantly the ones paying for pharmaceuticals with little chances to influence future research, the higher cost of pharmaceuticals is a key issue also in the developed countries.

The Commission in Intellectual Property Rights (CIPR) also warned that there may be problems in the future if the World Intellectual Property Organisation (WIPO) continues with its aims to harmonise substantive patent law. WIPO aims to promote intellectual property rights and makes no allowance for development considerations. Although the WIPO negotiations are at an early stage, there is a risk that some of the few flexibilities within the TRIPS agreement may be removed as part of the WIPO negotiations, for example, qualifications as to what constitutes a patentable invention or how the requirements of novelty, inventive step and industrial application are to be determined (CIPR 2002).

3.2.2 Policy advice from a health perspective

1. TRIPS agreement should be based – as stated in the agreement – on the balance between rights holders and consumers. The achievement of this balance requires a further reassessment of benefits and costs of the agreement.

2. Common concerns in health policies across countries need to be addressed. Flexibilities allowed in the TRIPS agreement should not be narrowed, but rather expanded in order to ensure that public health or human rights matters are not compromised to serve merely the interests of rights holders.

3. Rights to use compulsory licensing should not be narrowed in terms of restrictions on the basis of specific diseases, scope of economy or gravity of public health problems.

4. Nothing in the TRIPS agreement prohibits the use of parallel importing if a country applies international exhaustion of rights. The rights to use parallel importing in developing countries cannot be linked to availability of pharmaceuticals on tiered pricing.

5. It should be ensured that research and development efforts on health-related technologies are guided by health-related concerns and needs and not only market opportunities.

7. Investing development and health funds to corporate research and development efforts should be avoided or done carefully ensuring that intellectual property rights remains as public property.

8. On health and health policy grounds there are not reasons why test-data should not be disclosed as a condition for registering. The wording 'unfair' use can be interpreted in a very narrow sense.

9. Mechanisms to enhance developing country access to knowledge and information at low costs need to be sought as well as mechanisms ensuring free access to information and knowledge for educational, research and scientific purposes without fear of infringement of copyrights or intellectual property rights.

10. Developed countries should ensure that developing countries are not forced to excessive protection of intellectual property through bilateral treaties.

11. In addition to the TRIPS it may be important to focus to the WIPO as well. In this it is necessary to ensure that the WIPO harmonization of the substantive patent law around the world will take into account the interests of developing countries as well as other public interests beyond those of the rights holders.

3.3 The Agreement on the Application of Sanitary and Phytosanitary Measures (SPS)

3.3.1 SPS Agreement

The Agreement on the Application of Sanitary and Phytosanitary Measures (SPS) deals with food safety, and animal and plant health. It encourages WTO member countries to base their measures and regulations on international standards, guidelines and recommendations, where they exist. It recognises the right of governments to implement sanitary and phytosanitary measures, but stipulates that such measures must be based on science, should be applied only to the extent necessary to protect human or plant life or health, and should not arbitrarily or unjustifiably discriminate between members where identical or similar conditions prevail (WTO 1995). In practice, it means that any protectionist measures should not be "disguised" as measures to protect public health protection – but also means that public health measures can be accused of being protectionist. If a country implements stricter measures than international standards another country can challenge it to justify these measures.

In principle, the role of the SPS Agreement in trade disputes is in guiding sanitary and phytosanitary measures in general. It is linked with Article XX in the General Agreement on Tariffs and Trade (GATT) setting general exceptions to GATT rules (see 'International trade and health' in *Background* section earlier). The SPS Agreement elaborates on issues related to measures to protect animal, plant or human life or health (GATT 1994; Agreement on Application 1994). Thus, while governments have rights to implement sanitary and phytosanitary measures, such measures have to respect the stipulations set out in the SPS Agreement.

In recent years, increasing attention has been paid to the costs of implementing the SPS Agreement in developing countries. The World Bank research department has conducted studies, which claim that European countries are limiting the development options of developing countries by applying stricter standards than are required by Codex Alimentarius, the SPS's reference body (Otsuki et al 2001; Otsuki et al 2002). According to these studies, European public health regulations on pesticide residues on bananas and aflatoxins have led to developing countries losing earnings from trade in these products and therefore losing opportunities to trade and development.

The fear of protectionism may also result in problematic suggestions. In the case of bananas, it is hard to see regulations about pesticide residues as a protectionist measure because bananas do not grow in Europe to any significant extent. The pesticide regulation may also be regarded as a means to support banana growers who use less pesticides. Given that a higher use of pesticides is associated with larger plantations owned by multinational companies that tend to have fewer local benefits, it can be argued that Europe's stricter pesticide regulation will, in practice, shift European consumption towards supporting smaller farms which use less pesticides and thus could be claimed to support broader developmental impacts in general.

From a developing country perspective, it is clear that SPS implementation imposes additional costs and that stricter public health standards can be interpreted as barriers to trade. Indeed, any public health regulation could easily be challenged because it diminishes trade prospects of someone. However, the argument that public health regulations can constitute trade barriers to development is the start of a slippery downward slope towards deregulation. Thus emphasis on necessity clauses and role of public health regulations in restricting trade may easily trigger an unsustainable process of deregulation. Furthermore, the focus on developed country public health regulations as barriers to trade may in practice shift attention from other measures of much more direct and important trade distorting nature. Trade and industry proponents are usually not the greatest friends of public health regulations in the national context, considering public health regulations often as unnecessary government red tape. This bias leads easily to acceptance of public health regulations as the common problems in the sphere of trade policies.

The use of Codex standards as a reference point sounds sensible, but is in practice more problematic. When many of these standards were first established, it was not envisaged that Codex would become an international reference point and thus Codex standards tend to be less strict than those of public health regulations in developed countries. Industry has played a prominent role in Codex standard setting, compromising Codex's role as an impartial technical body. This has come about partly because of Codex's and partly because countries have chosen industry representatives for their national delegations. The role of industry was known already before the WTO (see e.g. Avery et al. 1993), but little has done to remedy the situation. It has further been noted, that in light of the new role of Codex under the SPS agreement, proceedings of the commission have often become trade battlegrounds and forums for deregulation. As a result recent Codex decisions reflect political compromises designed to promote international trade, not the best science to protect consumers (Silverglade 2000). However, compared to the International Standards Organisation (ISO), Codex is not an industry-run body, but is hosted jointly by WHO and FAO. Another concern in the context of the SPS has been seen in the potential expansion of ISO work to matters relevant of health. While it is hard to compare the structures and functions of different actors, one would assume that the Codex hosted by the UN agencies of the WHO and FAO, would form more developing country friendly environment in standard setting.

Implementation of the SPS Agreement can be regarded as a means to improve public health policies. When understood broadly it may be used as an incentive to upgrade and influence public health infrastructure and related practices in a country. But as a means it is far from an ideal solution because SPS covers only export products and does not apply to domestic trade and consumption. While SPS can be used to upgrade a broader set of policies, there is also a danger of putting too much emphasis on SPS may lead to streamlining export regimes rather than building up a national health and public health infrastructure or broader improvement in storage of food products or cattle raising and meat industry. Thus, focusing solely on SPS as means could also lead to worse national public health policies. The SPS does not require all imports to comply with it, but instead sets limits on what a government can and cannot restrict from being imported on the basis of health concerns. It is therefore not an optimal means of improving regulatory regimes in public health.

3.3.2 Health policy issues

As the costs of implementing the SPS agreement are becoming clearer to the developing world, and in anticipation of more trade in food products, it is quite probable that SPS-related arguments will be more on the agenda in future. It is highly likely that some proponents of more liberalised trade, such as the World Bank's research department on trade, and developing countries will regard developed country public health regulations as trade barriers. It is, however, important to consider the long-term consequences. It is crucial not to let trade-related arguments stamp all over health-related regulations, which should be assessed first and foremost in terms of their role in public health policies. After all, public health regulations will always restrict trade in some respect.

Proponents of trade liberalisation may put forward innovative views of how public health regulations should be changed so that they are more market friendly. But this is not their job nor their area of expertise. It is also likely that public health regulations designed by trade proponents will be more residual and lax than those drawn up by public health experts. It is also likely that the least trade restrictive means impose more costs and work to the public administration. There is thus a danger that an efficiency gained in trade policies results in further inefficiency in the public health administration.

The focus on public health regulations may also divert attention from other more important considerations in agricultural and food policies. The danger is that European public health regulations may be put to the fore to draw attention away from other measures, such as subsidies, which are at the core of the agricultural interests of the European Community and the United States.

It is clear that health arguments will be misused in trade debates. But the answer is not to undermine health arguments by instantly considering them to be protectionist measures. Instead, decision-making on substance matters should be shifted to forums which can deal authoritatively with the issue from a health perspective with equal access to the developing countries, such as UN organisations, other global intergovernmental bodies possibly or joint efforts with public health oriented public interest organisations in the area.

Another aspect is the role of aid in trade policies and the intersection of food and development policies. Aid may be given to a developing country to ensure that it supports to certain policy measures, which are of more relevance to European and US trade interests than development countries, for instance, the labelling of genetically modified foods, products and ingredients.

Future policy concerns are likely to focus on the nature and forums of standard setting. The work of the Codex Alimentarius Commission is likely to become highly pressured by commercial interests, which may not be conducive to an appropriate assessment of health considerations.

Increasing trade in food can be expected to lead to increasing problems of bacterial and viral epidemics merely because of longer transport-times and wider circulation. This will enhance pressures on public health regulations related to the quality of products and to inspections at the point of entry into a country.

3.3.3 Policy advice from a health perspective

The health policy arguments with respect to the SPS Agreement and related concerns can be summarised as follows:

1) The importance of public health regulatory measures as such and that these are not treated as merely protectionist measures in trade debates
2) The problematic basis of arguments on developmental gains of lowering public health regulations in long-term
3) The need of support to the developing world in enhancing their regulatory measures and doing so more broadly than merely in the context of the SPS
4) The role of the Codex Alimentarius commission and the necessity to ensure that scientific and public health concerns are of priority
5) The necessity to ensure that regulatory approaches such as the precautionary principle are not seen merely as a protectionist measure but a means to address certain public health policy concerns
6) The necessity to consider public health regulatory matters beyond product safety as well as those associated with production processes and the fact that this is going be criticized heavily by the developing world.

3.4. General Agreement on Trade in Services (GATS)

3.4.1 GATS Agreement and trade in services

The basic function of the General Agreement on Trade in Services is to liberalise international trade in services (GATS 1994). GATS permits government regulatory measures, but the context in which such measures are permitted and their scope is of concern. This is for the simple reason that domestic regulation is considered much more of a potential barrier to trade in services compared to trade in goods. Although regulation of service activities may imposed for purely domestic purposes, it almost always creates a powerful trade barrier. Trade in services is only affected by this and other non-tariff barriers; tariffs are totally absent (Sapir 1999). The essential aim of the GATS agreement is to regulate government actions within a framework of the progressive liberalisation of international trade in services. Liberalisation of service provision is expected to lead to benefits in broad terms as well as lower costs.

GATS outlines four "modes" or ways in which services can be provided internationally:

1) "cross-border supply of services";
2) "consumption abroad";
3) "commercial presence";
4) "presence of natural persons".

In terms of health services, international trade could encompass the following services:

1) services provided across national borders such as telemedicine or e-health and Internet services;
2) health tourism – that is, patients travelling to other countries to use the health care services there;
3) companies based in one country setting up a subsidiary or branch in another country in order to deliver the service in that country. This mode encompasses foreign investments in health care;
4) individuals from one country travelling to another country to supply a service there on a temporary basis, for example, nurses of doctors contracted to work in developed countries.

The role of mode 3 is by far the most important and has been calculated to account for the majority of trade in services. In health the modes 2 and 4 may be of importance as well, although the role of mode 4 has in general been negligible.

In the context of the ongoing GATS negotiations, specific concerns relate to:

1) safeguarding the role of public services;
2) domestic regulation in the context of regulatory reform;
3) the inclusion of government procurement practices; and
4) cross-subsidisation to maintain equity (financing, access to care/populations, areas)

Safeguarding the role of public services

The GATS agreement does have a basic exclusion from the Agreement for public services, but it is a very narrow clause. It excludes "any [government] service which is supplied neither on a commercial basis, nor in competition with one or more service providers". In most nation states, however, health services are not provided only by public entities; the majority are based on a mixture of public and private, non-profit and for-profit actors, as well as third party payers such as insurance companies.

The question of public services is thus at best unclear. According to the WTO secretariat free government provided services could not be challenged on the basis of GATS, however, the privatisation or commercialisation of these would automatically extend the application of the Agreement to these services (Adlung and Carzaniga 2001). It is also possible that commitments made under GATS to liberalise certain services in the private sector could also influence publicly-funded services provided by a private body on a contractual basis and charging a fee for services. Commitments could become contentious in the context of public support or grants to local non-profit organisations if these are not available for foreign private sector corporations or their non-profit affiliates. The mere existence EU horizontal exemption, which covers public services, is one example of the lack of sufficient trust on the interpretation and broadness of the exemption.

The role of national regulatory measures is of greater importance in international trade in services compared with trade in goods. Thus GATS supporters have continued to exert pressure to renegotiate and strengthen GATS Article VI covering domestic regulation as part of the unfinished agenda. There have also been interests for fast track, cluster or horizontal commitments, which all basically represent mechanisms to extend and deepen GATS coverage faster than the current process of sectoral and specific commitments (*see* e.g. Sauve and Stern 2000). These would also represent mechanisms to extend GATS coverage without thorough sectoral negotiations. The domestic regulation agenda is still open, but there have been interests to add more horisontal limitations to domestic regulations requiring further strengthening the emphasis on least trade restrictiveness, pro-competitiveness or requirement that regulations would be proportional to the required aim (see e.g. Pollock and Price 2000; Hoekman and Mattoo 2000; Sauve and Stern 2000).

It can be expected in future that countries will face pressure to include private sector services in their health, education and social services GATS commitments thus extending GATS coverage more to these sectors or part of them, such as hospitals or higher education. It is also possible that commitments made in bilateral negotiations may become a problem later due to the WTO broader requirement of most favoured nation principle as part of GATS, requiring the same treatment to any other foreign provider as one gives to the most favoured provider. This has been seen as a benefit for smaller developing country exporters benefiting from the lobbying power of larger actors, but it seems it may also be seen as a problem in areas where countries might wish to proceed in slow pace.

The possibility of including the plurilateral agreement on government procurement practices as part of GATS has gained varying support, but may be of importance in the context of health systems in which substantial part of services is contracted out and could be seen as one form of government procurement. While the prospects of including government procurement under GATS in the near future are slight, the European Commission sees this area as important because of its large economic share – government procurement covers about 15% of national budgets (European Commission 2001b, WTO 1999). The role of government procurement can be of special importance to the aims of cross-subsidisation across areas or to the relationship between local bodies and nongovernmental organisations, which may become put on the same line as corporate for-profit bodies or their non-profit affiliates. It may also be of more importance to developing countries than to the developed countries.

The European Community has emphasised the role of competition policies in the GATS negotiations and the need to ensure that regulations promote competition. This might result in promotion of pro-competitiveness requirements from the regulatory measures allowed under GATS as part of the negotiations on Article VI in the sectoral negotiations. In health systems, the main issue with respect to competition policies is that the requirements for the equal standing of public and private service providers in terms of maintenance, infrastructure costs and accounting may easily end up in bias towards private sector, fragment the organisation of health care and hinder more long-term perspectives.

It is estimated that the health services sector in the OECD countries alone account for US$ 3 trillion annually (Marconini 1998). While the developed countries have not been offensive in the area, it seems that some developing countries see prospects of broadening their access to the markets in the OECD countries. Both Mexico and India are searching out prospective markets, especially in supplying professional services (mode 4) in developed countries.

3.4.2 Health policy issues

The benefits of GATS are to a large extent based on the assumption of overall benefits of commercialisation and liberalisation of service provision. However, in health, education and social sectors there is less if any evidence on such efficiency gains and benefits from privatisation of service provision which would outweigh the costs or not compromise the aims of equity, continuity and sustainability of services provision. As the benefits claimed for the Agreement need to be weighted against the risks and problems which may result from opening up services to international trade, the estimated benefits and costs need to be clearly assigned to the relevant public or private sector. Given the current knowledge about the high costs of privatising health services and the problems in regulating the private providers of services (*see* e.g. Rice 1997, Evans 1997), it is not surprising that very few WTO member countries have made commitments under GATS to liberalise their health services. A background paper for the WHO Commission on Marcoeconomics and health has highlighted the problems with private health insurance and the challenges of developing countries with respect to private health insurance as the following: preventing the exclusion of the poor, 'dumping' of sick/expensive patients from private health plans to public services/streets, controlling health care costs and preserving the appropriate elements of the public health sector (such as broader preventive and curative programmes) (Sbarbaro 2000). In the light of these challenges and the limited regulatory capacities in most developing countries, it is unlikely that the benefits from infrastructure and knowledge transfer will benefit the public sector or those unable to purchase private insurance. Thus from the health policy point of view there is not very much to expect from trade in health insurance services for developing countries.

The WTO, however, has mostly dealt health services as equal to any other field of services. The secretariat had expressed hopes that prospects for trade in health services might change in future as more market-oriented reforms are implemented in the health sector in many countries through means other than GATS (WTO 1998c), although more recently WTO officials have also recognised the limits of international trade in health and social services (see e.g. Adlung and Carzaniga 2001).

The health policy issues raised by the GATS agreement relate not only to the health and social services sector but also to regulatory measures in other sectors, such as advertising of tobacco, alcohol and infant foods or the structure and access to other "services" such as water and sewage. It is quite possible that water and sewage services may become a much more important area in the development context due to larger current trade interests in the area.

The NGO community has become critical of water supply services. This has partly been fuelled by the Bolivian case (see e.g. Waskow 2002; Brettonwoods project 2002).

Bolivia contracted out the water supply of its largest city allegedly in association of World Bank lending resulting in higher water prices. The impact of the higher water prices on the access to water of those poor has caused concern. The investor left the country, but sued Bolivia on the basis of lost future earnings and brought the case to the World Bank International Centre for Settlement of Investment Disputes (ICSID). The lesson with respect to GATS and developing countries could be the difficulties of backing off badly negotiated or otherwise unsuccessful deals as well as possible problems if further investment aspects and rights of corporations to appeal are brought to the WTO as means of 'procedural fairness'.

It is highly likely that, if health services are liberalised under GATS, the gains are going to be marginal. The emphasis on access to new technologies is not simple. There are no reasons why developing countries would need more high cost technologies than developed ones and yet many developing countries have more CT and NMR scans than developed countries. Furthermore, when the new technologies are part of corporate hospitals catering merely for the highest national income section and foreign tourists, their relevance to national health system and especially those poorest is meagre. In comparison to freeing resources from the public sector, the existence of high-tech corporate sector in a country may in practice increase overall health care costs. The possibilities that GATS could be used to ensure that corporate hospitals provide 10% of beds to poorer patients have been presented. However, implementation of this is difficult to supervise with large possibilities of avoidance those with costly illnesses. Furthermore, the ethics of this proposal accepts that often more than 90% of the population would be served by the 10% of beds, while the 90% of beds would be reserved to often less than 10% of population and foreign tourists.

The regulatory capacities of countries are also of importance. There are little grounds for arguing that developing countries would benefit from further commercial involvement in their health care services as their capacities to deal with regulatory tasks are already overburdened. However, it is necessary to emphasise that requirements for regulatory action in order to maintain equity and quality are not equal to requirements for regulatory reform, which is driven more by the international corporate sector to ensure that the national regulatory environment is conducive to foreign investments. For many private investors markets in many developing countries are not yet regulated enough and the use of private health insurance is too low to guarantee sufficient profits. Instead, they are waiting for World Bank projects to bring about regulatory reform (Shekri 2001). The role of World Bank and IMF reforms as means for expansion of foreign investments in health services and insurance has caused concern already in the Latin America (Stocker et al 1999).

The regulatory aims of governments may and often should differ greatly from the needs of foreign investors especially if equity in access and financing of services is of importance. This means that any regulation is not good enough and that some regulatory measures, such as those geared to ensure – equity, efficiency and cost-containment, transparency and quality in service provision as well as access to services on the basis of need rather than ability to pay – may be far more difficult in a more commercialised environment than others, related more to business interests and environment. The problem with the GATS is that it tends to enhance the rights of the commercial actors in comparison to governments. It is often implied that developing countries would benefit from the regulatory structure of GATS and could add exemptions or requirements. But they can do this without making GATS commitments. The exemptions tend to be time-bound and also depend on capacities to negotiate them astutely. The downside is that under GATS, governments run the risk of their policies being locked into a multilateral framework driven by export and trade-interests and of having limited opportunities to alter them if the policies prove to be disadvantageous.

It is thus likely in principle that countries would benefit overall from keeping their health and social sectors outside of GATS. This does not prohibit trade or foreign investments in health care; it does mean, however, that countries have broader freedom to regulate and manage health sector. It is also failure to assume that diffusion of technology, knowledge, education and training or utilisation of new technologies such as telemedicine would and could be enhanced only via trade and commercial actors. International cooperation and research collaboration have broader relevance than that of trade. At the end of the day, GATS commitments would be important mostly if a country wanted to encourage private foreign investment and trade in health services in the country. It is unlikely that multinational private health services would improve the quality of national services or services for the poor. It is also arguable if benefits from GATS would be gained even in countries that already have privatised and corporatised health systems as their options to change the situation would then be locked to the GATS framework. The so called 'locked-in' nature of GATS makes it unwise to explore through commitments in areas where benefits are not clear. There is also a danger that in the process of enhancing foreign investments in health services, it would be the best performing national hospitals or those with the best reputation which would attract most foreign interest and become privatised as it is unlikely that the multinational corporate sector would be interested in the worst performing hospitals or those in remote areas.

It has been argued that health tourism (mode 2) and the export of health personnel (mode 4) could be a way in which developing countries could benefit from increased international trade in health care services (UNCTAD 1997). But this point of view tends to consider health care services mostly in the context of trade and the possibilities of increasing GDP. Health services have other more vital purposes, such as providing quality care for the sick, and preventive and promotive services to help people to become and to stay healthy. The focus on generating GDP easily leads to a bias in priorities and ineffectiveness in service provision within health system as a whole. There is also a risk that enhancing markets, profit incentives and health tourism in developing countries increases the risk of problematic operations, such as richer people buying organ transplants. Even the more positive assessments on trade in health services in the context of Indian already largely privatised health services and foreseeing many benefits associated with trade health services, have brought up the general perception that there have been adverse effects on the public health care system and on equity and that benefits have been limited to the affluent urban populations (see Chanda 2001).

Educating health professionals is relatively expensive, and many developing countries have a substantial lack of skilled personnel. It is unlikely that the export of an educated health workforce could be a desirable option for developing countries. However, export of health professionals has been a problem for many developing countries and may be estimated to increase in the context of GATS. It has been estimated that 56% of all migrating physicians come from developing countries and that the figure for nurses is likely to be higher. Among doctors it is often the categories that are in short supply which go abroad. Although skilled health personnel tend to go to the industrial countries of North, there is also a considerable South-South flow. (Adams and Kinnon 1998). The magnitude of this is substantial extending in some countries such as Pakistan to up to 50% of the graduates (see e.g. Chanda 2001). The "brain drain" of skilled workers from many countries is often problematic anyway; the value of the remittances they send back is minor in comparison to the loss of potential earnings. Further brain drain of skilled workers is clearly an issue, especially as some countries, such as India, have seen broader opportunities for themselves in this mode.

If barriers to the movement of health personnel are reduced without an appropriate regulatory framework and/or improvement in working and income conditions in the domestic health system, equity, quality and efficiency will all suffer. However, it is worth noting that GATS places limitations on the presence of persons supplying services and its provisions apply to people who supply services abroad on fixed term, rather than on a permanent basis (Orvill and Kinnon 1998). The GATS covers trade in professional services separately and the mode 4 implies a temporary movement of persons as part of broader contract. The role of the mode 4 matters as well as on trade in professional services will most probably unfold in more detailed discussions. This could most probably include also the further negotiation on matters related to economic needs tests, licensing and other regulatory measures limiting trade prospects and movement of persons.

If countries would decide to invest on health tourism as a new trade and industry area, the limits of this are defined by the portability of health insurance in the developed countries (see e.g. Warner 1998). The promotion of trade in health and health services at global level may also lead to ethical problems with diffusion of questionable health procedures and practices to countries with least regulatory interference. The matter of concern can be illustrated through the prospects of enhancing transplant services in the developing world, where the regulatory environment may allow human body parts to be bought or otherwise gained from grey sources more easily. A liver transplant costs only one tenth of the costs in the US when done in India (Chanda 2001). The fear is that easily accessible livers may become merely a part of the costs – a comparative advantage – and acquired without an appropriate consent or at worst through criminal activities. There is a scarcity in organ transplants and already a concern over illegitimate trade in human body parts. The more global health services become, the more legitimate concerns over possible problems and ethical concerns need to be taken into account.

In many countries health insurance and pensions have been the areas in which GATS interests have been strongest. The possibilities of GATS to enhance the expansion of private insurance has been considered as one of the more problematic aspects of the agreement due to regulatory difficulties and risk of cream-skimming of those affluent and healthy by the private sector with the consequence that public resources and capacities to cater for those ill and poor would be even more compromised.

The role of broader public health policies is as important in the developing world as it is in developed countries. This applies particularly to the advertising and marketing of products that hazardous to health, such as alcohol or tobacco or that have the effect of discouraging healthy practices such as breastfeeding. While WHO's Code on the marketing of breast-milk substitutes and infant foods provides some support for maintaining restrictions on the marketing and promotion of infant foods and WHO's forthcoming framework convention on tobacco control may well do the same with respect to tobacco, GATS commitments in advertising services could be used against these limitations on the free movement of advertising services. The matter dealing with a similar issue in the context of internal markets regulations has been raised at the European Court of Justice in a case involving Sweden's restriction on alcohol advertising (European Court of Justice 2001, Grieshaber-Otto and Schacter 2001). It is probable that pressure on the matter could be brought to bear on developing countries by the relevant industries, even when there would be no real threat of a dispute being taken to the WTO. It would therefore benefit developing countries in particular if the rights of governments to restrict advertising on the basis of public health and social concerns were reiterated.

The best option seems to be that health and social services should stay outside GATS commitments. But for those countries which have already committed substantial service sectors, there are options, which could be added to GATS during the current negotiations to ensure that governments maintain certain core functions without other countries being able to request compensation from them for the economic impact of these measures. For instance, mechanisms to ensure that a government has some capacity to address inequalities between regions or population groups are found in US exceptions for subsidies to poorer populations, and the EU's horizontal exceptions for public services. It is unlikely, although not impossible, that these countries should prohibit the use of similar exclusions by the developing world. It is also likely that the current negotiations could provide an entry for the developing countries to require similar rights as part of the negotiation process with little moral high ground for the developed countries to argue against these. They also reflect the vagueness and insufficiency of the WTO public services exemption discussed earlier in this brief.

As GATS mandates progressive service liberalisation through successive rounds of negotiations, future policy concerns relate primarily to the prospects of countries opening and deepening their commitments under GATS and thereby extending their commitments to health and social services. Of particular importance will be the negotiations and proposals into making horizontal commitments (that is, those that cover all service sectors) and proposals to introduce more specific requirements for domestic regulation (see e.g. Hoekman and Mattoo 2000). It is unclear how data disclosure is treated in GATS, nor to what extent pressures are being exerted to introduce different "necessity" clauses into domestic regulation, for example that the measure must be in proportion to its anticipated impact. Proportionality measures may have the effect of limiting broader public policies and regulatory options for health purposes.

The European Commission and other partners have promoted the role of e-health/ electronic health services/internet trade in health and telemedicine (see e.g. Lamy 2001). Developing countries could benefit from these services as such, especially in being more able to obtain up-to-date information, to access data on health matters, and to enable people in more remote areas to have health consultations. But it is unlikely that the liberalisation of health services trade would fuel these benefits and there is a danger that the potential benefits could be diminished due to further commercialisation of internet services and increasing costs of knowledge distributed through the net. While the main limit for the developing world may have so far been the cost of technology, the further commercialisation of the internet and provision of information through it may diminish the importance of the internet as source of knowledge in future. The prospects for telemedicine in developing countries have been seen as promising especially for remote areas and advisory services. The dilemma again is to what extent this would gain from commercial and trade activity and to what extent benefits should and could be seen more as part of international cooperation.

There is a risk that all international exchanges are seen merely as trade and commercial activity, when their relevance is much more related to rather more traditional collaboration and knowledge sharing. Furthermore, when these would technically represent commercial activity it is not self-evident that commercial regulations are always the most conducive in all sectors in enhancing knowledge sharing. The overemphasis on commercial aspects may result in international consultations limited to individual corporations and their international counterparts and costly internet services with little relevance to poorer sections of society.

3.4.3 Policy advice from a health perspective

The main policy advice from a health policy perspective is to keep health and social services out of GATS commitments. It is unlikely that further commitments would provide additional gains but more likely that, if countries proceed along this route and found them costly or detrimental, it would be difficult for them to retract, especially in countries where there are substantial prospects for commercial health services.

Once countries have already made commitments, the focus needs to be on the interpretation of GATS and on ensuring that commitments are interpreted in a sense which is supportive to broader public policies and regulatory requirements in health. Countries could also try to use some exemption mechanisms used by the US and the European Community.

GATS commitments are likely to be irrelevant, or at least of minor interest, to many of the poorest developing countries. These countries are likely to consider any foreign investment in health as an improvement. But it is also likely that GATS commitments would have little or nothing to do with any foreign involvement in health services in these countries. Instead, such services would be much more dependent on aid and other flows of resources.

Countries should not take as granted the GATS exemption of public services to cover all health services. In domestic regulation necessity, proportionality or pro-competitiveness requirements should be avoided as well as any commitments meant to reach beyond a specific sector.

The costs and benefits of mode 3 liberalisation are of major importance especially as the other modes represent more marginal share of trade. Benefits of technology change and infrastructure improvements need to be set against costs and accessibility of services. It is unlikely that corporate investments would be made to focus on those poor and unable to pay, thus usually either relying on government reimbursement of costs or the richer sections of society.

'Brain drain' has been defined as a major risk with respect to trade in health services. While it is generally waste of developing countries, it is nothing new. There are little grounds to enhance the drain of skilled population from the developing countries and remittances back home rarely cover the lost skills and capacities.

In terms of trade policies and options for developing countries, caution is the operative word. Cautiousness should also be extended to services that are of major importance to the determinants of health, such as water and sewage treatment services.

4. European policies, trade, development and health

4.1 Health policy issues

European policies have an impact on health and trade considerations in several ways. The European Commission is involved in the practical day-to-day work of negotiating the WTO agreements and in many cases represents the EU Member States at crucial stages. These include the negotiations of bilateral treaties, which are often done in much more hurried time-scale and run the risk of introducing sectoral commitments beyond current GATS commitments if adequate care is not taken.

There has been an increasing emphasis on making European Community policies coherent and on speaking with "one voice" in all external policies (European Commission 2001c). This has benefits, but also dangers, if it makes easier to compromise development interests by stronger trade interests and reduce development policies to a means to fill gaps or needs in trade policies. One example of this is the use of aid funds to develop and procure pharmaceuticals, a crucial part of the EU's poverty reduction and development programme launched in 2000 (European Commission 2001a).

In trade policies many social and development aspects are presumed to be conveyed by the civil society consultations. The problem of these consultations is the dominance of corporate and single issue actors in the consultations. In development matters there is also a concern that substance-related health or education policy aspects become undermined by larger debates on agricultural subsidies as very few NGOs focus on the substance areas of health and social policies. The matter of access to pharmaceuticals has been high also on the European agenda due to two strong actors, the Medecins sans Frontiers and the OXFAM, lobbying actively on the matter (see e.g. www.msf.org, www.oxfam.org). In the development NGO sphere the Save the Children Fund has profiled with broadest and most comprehensive agenda on trade in services and specific focus also on health services (see e.g. Hilary 2001). Other European NGO networks and campaigns with focus on trade include S2B- Seattle to Brussels – network with active involvement of Friends of the Earth and the Transnational Institute and focus on GATS (see e.g. www.gatswatch.org). Health was first raised to the European agenda on 2000 through a broad NGO seminar on health and trade organised by the European Public Health Alliance (EPHA), however, since then the role of health oriented NGOs in trade matters has been more limited. The forums of TACD and TABD are important in discussing and debating EU policies on trade and trade-related matters (see www.tacd.org). This is partly related to the fact that some of the American consumer organisations have been particularly active on matters of TRIPS and GATS (see e.g. www.cptech.org).

The participation and engagement with civil society dialogues is important, but not sufficient to guarantee appropriate policy choices. One problem with the current practice civil society participation tends to be that these are often burdened by requirements of campaigning and evidence of result, gearing activities towards single issues or diseases, which are not always conducive to health policy contents in practice.

The European Community does not have competence on health and social services because, on the basis of the subsidiarity principle, these are matters for national decision-making. It is important to ensure that when the Commission is making its trade policies and requests to other countries that such offensives do not compromise health and social policies or the goal of poverty reduction. The lack of attention to the matters at European level may further pave away to problematic requests in the context of trade offensives.

In the European Community, intellectual property rights and pharmaceutical issues are negotiated on a Community basis. The Nice intergovernmental conference gave the Commission competency only in the area of commercial aspects of intellectual property rights. However, public health related matters are fundamentally broader. European Commission stands on intellectual property rights are dominated by the interests those of rights holders. This has lead to the rather paradoxal state of European policies compromising in practice the actual needs of health policies in Europe.

4.2 Advice from health policy perspective

In many health issues common developmental and health policy perspectives can be found with capacities to support stands and strengthen the relevance of these viewpoints especially when views of trade proponents are contrasting or represent mostly industry interests.

The consultation times of European Commission documents are usually very short and the role of various actors unclear. There is a danger of drowning other partners in papers to be commented and consequently of lack capacity to follow and understand actual processes of trade negotiations and priorities and yet giving the impression that substance matters have been consulted.

The coherence of European external policies should not be achieved through making aid and development policies to follow European trade priorities.

The European civil society consultations have an inbuilt bias towards larger and more 'European' actors. Care should be taken to avoid that these forums are overtaken by business interests. Due to the nature of trade negotiations and importance of knowing export interests, the key trade forums and committees in the Commission are more accessible to industry actors than to the NGOs. Transparency beyond invited committee meetings could be further enhanced.

In development and health issues a broader European view beyond industrial interests would be welcome, covering views of European parliament, Member State public policy priorities as well as views of civil society organisations working on health and development. The danger is that current European processes seem to enhance the bias that European interests are assumed as the same as European export industry interests.

Acknowledgements

I would like to thank Minna Ilva for her thorough work on the policy briefs during the year, Sarah Sexton for editing and much more as well as helpful and insightful comments from my co-workers on the first drafts.

References

Abbot FM. (2002), "The Doha declaration on the TRIPS agreement and public health: lighting a dark corner at the WTO", *Journal of International Economic Law* 469–505.

Actionaid (2002), *Farmgate. The developmental impact of agricultural subsidies.* Actionaid, United Kingdom.

Adams O, Kinnon C. (1998), A public health perspective. In: Zarrilli S, Kinnon C (eds): *International trade in health services. A development perspective.* UNITED NATIONS/UNCTAD and WHO, Geneva

Adlung R, Carzaniga A (2001), "Health services under the general agreement on trade in services", *World Health Bulletin* vol. 79, no. 4. pp. 352– 364

Agreement on application of sanitary and physosanitary measures. (SPS Agreement). (1994) Marrakesh, April 15, 1994.

Agreement on Trade-related Aspects of Intellectual Property Rights (TRIPS Agreement). (1994) Marrakesh, April 15, 1994.

Ahn, D. (2000), "Linkages between international financial and trade institutions. IMF, World Bank and the WTO". *Journal of World Trade* vol. 34, no. 4, pp. 1–36.

Avery N, Drake M, Lang T. (1993), *Cracking the Codex*, National Food Alliance, London.

Barnum, H. (1994), "The economic burden of the global trade in tobacco", *Tobacco Control* vol. 3, pp. 358–361.

Bettcher, D., Yach, D., Guindon, E. (2000), "Global trade and health: key linkages and future challenges," *Bulletin of the World Health Organisation* vol. 78, no. 4, pp. 521–534.

Braithwaite, J., Drahos, P. (2000), *Global business regulation.* Cambridge University Press.

Brettonwoods project (2002), *World Bank pushed to open up Bolivia water arbitration* [online] available: www.brettonwoodsproject.org/topic/privatesector/p3001bolivia.html

Butler D. (1998a), "World Bank calls for fairer deal on patents and knowledge", *Nature* vol. 395, pp. 529.

Butler D, Spurgeon D. (1997), "Canada and France fall out over the risks of asbestos", *Nature* vol. 358, pp. 379.

Chanda, R. (2001), *Trade in health services*, CMH Working paper series. Paper no WG 4:5. Commission on Macroeconomics and Health.

Cook P, Kirkpatrick C. (1995), *Globalisation, regionalisation and third world development* (mimeo). University of Manchester and University of Bradford, cited in UNCTAD. Least developed countries 1996 report. UNCTAD, Geneva.

CIPR (2002) *Integrating intellectual property rights and development Policy*. Commission on Intellectual Property Rights. London, September. [online] available: www.ipr.com

Correa CM.(2000), "Implementing national public health policies in the framework of WTO agreements." *Journal of World Trade* vol. 34, no. 5, pp. 89–121.

Correa CM (2002a), *Implications of the Doha Declaration on the TRIPS Agreement and Public Health*, Health Economics and Drugs EDM Series No 12, WHO/EDM/PAR/2002.3.

Correa, C.M. (2002b), *Protection of data submitted for the registration of pharmaceuticals: implementing the standards of the TRIPS agreement*. South Centre in Collaboration with Department of Essential Drugs and Medicines Policy, World Health Organisation.

Drahos P. (1995), "Global Property rights in information. The story of TRIPS and the GATT", *Prometheus*, vol. 13, no. 1, pp. 6–19.

Drahos P. (1997), "Thinking strategically about intellectual property rights" *Telecommunications Policy* vol 21:3:201–211.

Drahos P. (1999), *Biotechnology, patents, markets and morality*, Essays on Intellectual Property Rights issues. Sweet and Maxwell ltd., pp.441–447

Drahos, P. (2001), *Bilateralism in intellectual property*. A commissioned Oxfam policy paper. December 2001. [online] available: www.oxfam.co.uk/policy/papers/bilateral/bilateral.html

Eisma D. (1999), How to build a better EU health budget. *Eurohealth* vol. 5, pp. 12–13.

English P, Hoekman BM, Mattoo A. (2002), *Development, Trade and the WTO: A Handbook*, World Bank, Washington DC, [online] available: www.worldbank.org

European Commission (2001a), *Communication from the Commission to the action on HIV/AIDS, malaria and tuberculosis in the context of poverty reduction*. EN/D/347.2001.

European Commission (2001b), *EC Approach to Government Procurement*, April 2000. [online] available: www.europa.eu.int/comm/trade/miti/gov_proc/seaproc.htm. (Accessed 11.09.2001)

European Commission (2001c), Commission staff working document. *The European Community's Development policy*. Programme of Action. Commission of the European Communities, Brussels, 26 January 2001. SEC(2001)150.

European Court of Justice (2001), Case C–405/98. *Konsumentombudsmannen v. Gourmet International Products Aktiebolag*. Judgement of the court 8 March 2001.

European Parliament (2002), The text adopted by the European Parliament for an amendment to the DIRECTIVE 2001/83/EC OF THE EUROPEAN PARLIAMENT AND OF THE COUNCIL of 6 November 2001 on the Community code relating to medicinal products for human use. European Parliament. Text adopted Wednesday 23 October. PE 323.680.

Evans, R.G. (1997), Going for the gold. The re-distributive agenda behind the market-based health care reform, *Journal of Health Politics, Policy and Law* vol.22, pp. 427-465.

Fidler DF. (1997), "Trade and Health: The global spread of diseases and international trade", *German Yearbook of International Law*, 40.

Final report (2000), Final report for the DG Trade of European Commission submitted by CEAS Consultants in Association with Geoff Tansey and Queen Mary Intellectual Property Research Institute, *Study on the relationship between the Agreement on TRIPS and biodiversity related issues,* September 2000, [online] available: www.europa.eu.int

Finger, M., Schuler, P. (1999), *"Implementation of Uruguay Round Committments: the Development challenge"*. [Online] available: www1.worldbank.org/wbiep/trade/documents/UR_commit.pdf

Food First Institute (2002), *Statement to the WTO Director General on the Agreement on Agriculture,* 13 November 2002 [online] available: www.foodfirst.org/progs/global/trade/wto2001/agletterwto.html

GATT (1994), General Agreement on Tariffs and Trade (1947) (as amended through 1966)

GATS (1994), General Agreement on Trade in Services (GATS Agreement). Marrakesh, April 15, 1994.

Grieshaber-Otto, J and Schacter, N. (2001), "Impacts of the international "services" treaty on health-based alcohol regulation", *Nordisk alcohol & narkotikatidskrift* vol. 18, no. 3. [online] available: www.stakes.fi/nat/english/articles.htm

Griesgraber JM, Gunter BG. (1997), *World Trade: Towards fair and free trade in the twenty-first century,* Pluto Press, London.

Haaparanta, P. (2001), *Yhdentyvä maailmantalous ja sen seuraukset.* Studia Generalia -luento 4.10.2001, Helsingin Kauppakorkeakoulu.

Hilary, J. (2001), *The Wrong Model. GATS , trade liberalisation and public health,* Save the Children, London.

Held, D, McGrew A, Goldblatt D, Perraton J. (1999), *Global transformations. Politics, Economics and Culture,* Cambridge, Polity.

Hirst OP, Thompson G. H. (1996), *Globalisation in question,* Polity Press, Cambridge.

Hoekman B, Kostecki M. (1997), *The Political Economy of the World Trading System.* Oxford University Press, Oxford. 1997.

Hoekman B, Mattoo A (2000), "Services, economic development and the next round of negotiations on services" *Journal of International Development* vol. 12, pp. 283–296.

Khor, M. (1997), "The World Trade Organisation and the south: fighting back the tide" *Development* vol. 40 no. 4, pp. 73-77.

Khor M. (1999), "WTO must resolve issues of transparency and participation" *Third World Resurgence,* vol. 104/105, pp. 41–44.

Kneen B. (1995), *Invisible Giant: Cargill and its transnational strategies,* Pluto Press and Fernwood Publishing, London. .

Koivusalo M, Ollila E. (1997), *Making a healthy world,* Zed books, London.

Koivusalo M. (1999), *World Trade Organisation and trade-creep in health and social policies,* GASPP Occasional Papers 4, STAKES, Helsinki. [online] available: www.gaspp.org/publications

Koivusalo M. (2001), *Code and the WTO,* A briefing paper for the WEMOS and IBFAN meeting on trade and infant feeding, CRASH paper no 1. September 2001, [online] available: www.crash.kaapeli.fi (in process).

Kwa, A. (2002), *Power Politics in the WTO,* Focus on the Global South, Bangkok. [online] available: www.focusweb.org

Lamy P. (2000), "Health services and international trade: the role of the European Commission", *Eurohealth* vol. 6, no. 4, pp. 14–15.

Marceau G, Pedersen PN. (1999), "Is the WTO Open and Transparent? A Discussion of the Relationship of the WTO with Non-governmental Organisations and Civil Society's Claims for more Transparency and Public Participation" *Journal of World Trade* 1999, vol. 33, no.1, pp. 5–49.

Marconini M. (1998), Domestic capacity and international trade in health services: the main issues, In:

Zarrilli S, Kinnon C (eds), *International trade in health services. A development perspective.* UNITED NATIONS/UNCTAD and WHO, Geneva.

McNeil DG. (2001), "Profits on cosmetic save cure for sleeping sickness", *New York Times* 9 February 2002.

Mokhiber R. (1996), "Gerber uses threat of GATT sanctions to gain exemption from Guatemalan infant health law", *Corporate Crime Reporter* 19, [online] redistributed in: http://essential.org/cpt/ip/gerber/txt. (Accessed 23 August 1997).

Otsuki T, Wilson J (2001), *Global trade and food safety: winners and losers ina fragmented system,* Working Paper 2689, 1 October, World Bank, [Online] available: http://econ.worldbank.org/files/1424_wps2689.pdf

Otsuki T, Wilson J. (2002), *To spray or not to spray ? Pesticides, banana exports and food safety,* Working paper 2805, 21 March ,World Bank. [online] available: http://econ.worldbank.org/files/1424_wps2805.pdf

Oxfam (2002a), *Boxing match in agricultural trade,* Oxfam briefing paper 32, Oxfam, United Kingdom, [online] available: www.oxfam.co.uk/policy/papers/32trade/32trade.html

Oxfam (2002b), *Stop the dumping* ! Oxfam briefing paper 31, [online] available: www.oxfam.co.uk/policy/papers/31dumping/31dumping.html

Oxfam (2002c), *The great EU Sugar Scam.* Oxfam briefing paper 27. [online] available: www.oxfam.co.uk/policy/papers/27sugar/27sugar.html

Oxfam (2002d), *US bullying on drug patents.* Oxfam briefing paper 33. [online] available: www.oxfam.co.uk/policy/papers/33bullying/33bullying.html

Palmedo M. (2001), *Adrian Otten missive on WTO/WHO cooperation. 21 September 2001.* [online] available: http://lists.essential.org/pipermail/ip-health/2001-september/001892.html.

Phillips PWB, Kerr WA. (2000), Alternative Paradigms. The WTO versus the Biosafety Protocol for Trade in Genetically Modified Organisms. *Journal of World Trade* vol. 34, no.4, pp. 64–75.

Philip Morris (2001), *Submission by Philp Morris International inc. in response to the national centre for standards and certification information.* Foreign trade notification NO.G/TBT/N/CAN/22.

Pollock A, Price D. (2000), "Rewriting the regulations: How the World Trade Organisation could accelerate privatisation in health-care systems" *Lancet* vol. 356, pp. 1995–2000.

Rice T. (1997), "Can markets give us the health system we want", *Journal of Health Politics, Policy and Law,* vol. 22, pp.383–426.

Rodrik D. (2001), *The Global governance of trade as if development really mattered..* UNDP Background paper.UNDP, New York. [online] available: www.undp.org.

Sapir, A. (1999), "The General Agreement in Trade in Services. From 1994 to 2000", *Journal of World Trade,* vol. 33,no. 1, pp.51–66.

Sauve P, Stern RM (eds) (2000), *GATS 2000. New directions in services trade liberalisation.* Washington DC: Brookings Institution Press.

Sbarbaro JA. (2000), *Trade liberalisation in health insurance: Opportunities and challenges: The potential impact of introducing or expanding the availability of private insurance within low and middle income countries.* CMH Working Paper Series, Paper WG 4:6. [online] available: www.cmhealth.org.

Scholte, J.A. , O'Brien R, Williams M.(1999), "The WTO and Civil Society", *Journal of World Trade,* vol, 33, no.1, pp.107–123.

Sekhri N. (2000), India, in: Wieners, W.W. (ed) *Global Healthcare markets. A comprehensive guide to regions, trends and opportuniteis shaping the international health arena,* Jossey-Bass, San Fransisco. .

Sharma, R. (2002), *Developing country experience with the WTO agreement on agriculture and negotiationg and policy issues*. Paper presented at the International Agricultural Trade Research Consortium (IAYTC) summer symposium on the Developing Countries, Agricultural Trade and the WTO. Whistler Valley, Vancouver, Canada. 16–17 June 2002.

Shiva, V. (2001), *Protect or plunder. Understanding intellectual property rights*, Zed books, London.

Silverglade, B. (2000) *The WTO Agreement on Sanitary and Phytosanitary Measures – Weakening Food safety Regulation to Facilitate Trade.* Seminar Paper 25 May 2000 Amsterdam, Netherlands.

Stewart, F. (1995), Biases in global markets: can the forces of inequity and marginalisation be modified, In: Ul Haq M, Jolly R, Streeten P and Haq K (eds) *The UN and the Bretton Woods Institutions. New Challenges for the Twenty-First Century*, MacMillan, London.

Stern, N. (2002), *Cutting agricultural subsidies.* Speech at the Center for Economic Studies, Munich. 20 November [online] available: www.worldbank.org

Stocker, K., Waitzkin, H., Iriart, C. (1999), "The exportation of managed care to Latin America." *New England Journal of Medicine* vol. 340, pp. 1131–1136

South Centre (1997a), *Foreign direct investment, development and the new global economic order,* Atar, Geneva.

Tarabusi, CC, Vickery, G. (1998), Globalisation in the pharmaceutical industry. *International Journal of Health Services* vol. 28, pp. 67–105.

Third World Network (2001), The multilateral trading system: a development perspective. December 2001. UNDP Background papers. [online] available: www.undp.org/mainundp/propoor/docs/TWN%20text%20jan11.pdf

UNCTAD (1997), *International trade in health services: difficulties and opportunities for developing countries,* UNCTAD TD/B/COM1/EM.1/2. 7 April 1997. GE 97–50672.

UNCTAD (1996), *The least developed countries report 1996*, UNCTAD, Geneva.

UNCTAD (2002a), *Trade and development report 2002*, UNCTAD, Geneva.

UNCTAD (2002b), *The least developed countries report 2002*, UNCTAD, Geneva.

Understanding on Rules and Procedures Governing the Settlement of Disputes,. (1994) Marrakesh, April 15. 1994.

UNDP (1997*), Human Development Report*, Oxford University Press, Oxford.

UNDP (2001), *Human Development Report*, Oxford University Press, Oxford.

United Nations (2001a), *The impact of the Agreement on Trade-Related Aspects of Intellectual Property Rights on human rights,* Report of the High Commissioner, E/CN.4/Sub.2/20001/13, 27 June 2001. 53rd Session of the Sub-Commission on the Promotion and Protection of Human Rights.

United Nations (2001b), Commission on Human Rights. *Intellectual Property Rights and Human Rights.* Report of the Secretary General. E/CN.4/Sub.2/2001/12. 14 June 2001.

van der Stichele M. (1998), *Towards a world transnationals organisation ?* WTO Booklet series, vol. 3. Transnational Institute, 30 April 1998.

Warner, D. (1998), The globalisation of medical care. In: Zarrilli, S. and Kinnon, C. (eds), *International trade in health services. A development perspective.* UNITED NATIONS/UNCTAD and WHO, Geneva.

Waskow D. (2002), *Thirst for profit: are major corporations fit to deliver water to the World.* September 24. [online] available: www.foe.org/site1/act/thirst.html

Velasquez, G., Boulet, P. (1997), *Globalisation and access to drugs. Implications of the WTO/TRIPS Agreement,* WHO/DAP/98.9. Health Economics and Drugs. DAP Series No. 7. WHO, Geneva.

WHO (1981), *International Code of Marketing of Breast-milk Substitutes*, WHO, Geneva.

WHO (1998a), Resolution of the Executive Board, EB 101.R24, WHO, Geneva.

WHO (1998b), *Revised Drug Strategy. WHO's work in pharmaceuticals and essential drugs*, EB/RDS/

RC/1, WHO, Geneva.

WHO (1999*)*, Public health and trade. Comparing the role of the three international organisations, *Weekly epidemiological record* vol. 25, pp.193–208.

Winters, LA. (2002), Trade policies for poverty alleviation, in: English P, Hoekman B, Mattoo A (eds) *Development, trade and the WTO: A handbook,* World Bank, Washington DC.

WTO (1995), *Trading for the future*, World Trade Organisation, Geneva.

WTO (1996), *Japan – taxes on alcoholic beverages. Dispute settlement body*, Apellate body report and Panel report, WTO, Geneva.

WTO (1998a), *European Communities - Measures Affecting the Prohibition of Asbestos and Asbestos Products, complaint by Canada*, WT/DS135. World Trade Organisation, Geneva.

WTO (1998b), *Health and Social Services.* Council for Trade in Services, S/C/W/50, 18 September 1998. WTO, Geneva.

WTO (1999), *Overview of the Agreement on Government Procurement*, WTO, Geneva. [online] available: http://www.wto.org/wto/govt/over.htm. (Accessed May 4, 1999)

WTO (2001), *European Communities Measures affecting asbestos and asbestos-containing products.*Appellate body report and panel report – action by the dispute settlement body. WT/DS/135/12.

WTO (2001), *Declaration on the TRIPS Agreement and public health.* [online] available: www.wto.org/ english/thewto_e/minist_e/min01_e/mindecl_trips_e.htm WT/MIN01/DEC/2.20 November 2001.

WTO (2002), *What is the WTO. Fact file*, [online] available: www.wto.org/english/thewto_e/whatis_e/ whatis_e.htm

WTO/WHO (2002), *WTO Agreements and public health. A joint study by the WHO and the WTO secretariat*, WTO/WHO, Geneva.

ANNEX 1

Implications of the Doha declaration on the TRIPS Agreement and public health.

Executive summary

1. The adoption of the Doha Ministerial Declaration on TRIPS and Public Health was the outcome of carefully elaborated strategy by developing countries and a significant achievement of those nations.

2. The Doha Declaration recognises the 'gravity' of the public health problems afflicting many developing and LDCs, especially those resulting from HIV/AIDS, tuberculosis, malaria and other epidemics. But the Declaration reflects the concerns of developing countries and LDCs about the implications of TRIPS agreement with regard to public health in general, without limitation to certain diseases.

3. While acknowledging the role of intellectual property protection 'for the development of new medicines', the Declaration specifically recognises concerns about its effects on prices.

4. The Declaration affirms that ' the TRIPS Agreement does nott and should not prevent Members from taking measures to protect public health' and that it should be interpreted accordingly.

5. In establishing that Public Health is a clearly stated purpose of the Agreement, the Doha Declaration establishes a specific rule of interpretation that gives content to general interpretive provisions of the Vienna Convention on the Law of the Treaties on which GATT/WTO jurisprudence has been built up. Therefore, in cases of ambiguity, panels and the Appellate Body should opt for interpretations that are effectively 'supportive of WTO Members right to protect public health'.

6. The confirmation that the TRIPS Agreement has left room for flexibility at the national level has important political and legal implications. It indicates that the pressures to impede the use of available flexibilities run counter to the spirit and the purpose of the TRIPS Agreement. In legal terms, it means that panels and the Appellate body must interpret the Agreement and the laws and regulations adopted to implement it in the light of the public health needs of individual Members.

7. The Declaration clarifies that 'public health crises' can represent 'a national emergency or other circumstances of extreme urgency' and that an 'emergency' may either be a short-term problem, or a long-lasting situation. The Declaration also places the burden on complaining Member to prove that an emergency or urgency does not exist.

8. The Doha Declaration clarifies Members right to adopt an international principle of exhaustion of rights (determining the rules by which parallel imports may be accepted). The declaration states that 'the effect of the provisions in the TRIPS Agreement ….is to leave each Member free to establish its own regime for such exhaustion without challenge'.

9. The Declaration recognises an unresolved problem relating to TRIPS and Public Health - the use of compulsory licensing with countries with little or no manufacturing capacity or insufficient market demand - and commits the governing body of the TRIPS, the TRIPS Council to reach a solution by 2002.

10. In considering various approaches to the problem of compulsory licensing in countries with little of no manufacturing capacity or insufficient market demand, Members must be mindful of choosing an approach that provides adequate incentives for the production and export of the medicines in need.

11. Desirable features of any possible solution to the problem of compulsory licensing in countries with little of no manufacturing capacity or insufficient market demand would include: a stable international legal framework; transparency and predictability of the applicable rules in the exporting and importing countries; simple and speedy legal procedures in the exporting and importing countries; equality of opportunities for countries in need of medicines, even for products not patented in the importing country; facilitation of a multiplicity of potential suppliers of the required medicines from the developed and developing countries; and a broad coverage in terms of health problems and the range of medicines.

12. The Doha Declaration permits LDCs to opt for an extension of the transitional period provided for under the Article 66.1 of the TRIPS Agreement in relation to pharmaceutical patents. However, because all but few LDCs already grant patent protection to pharmaceuticals, this apparent concession to LDCs may have little practical effect.

13. It is implicit within the Doha Declaration that differentiation in patent rules may be necessary to protect public health. The singling out of public health, and in particular pharmaceuticals, as an issue needing special attention in TRIPS implementation constitutes recognition that public health-related patents may be treated differently than other patents.

14. The Doha Declaration is a strong political statement that can make it easier for developing countries to adopt measures necessary to ensure access to health care without the fear of being dragged into a legal battle. The Declaration is also a Ministerial decision with legal effects on the Members and on the WTO bodies, particularly the Dispute Settlement Body and the Council for TRIPS.

Source: Correa C. (2002), *Implications of the Doha Declaration on the TRIPS Agreement and Public Health.* Health Economics and Drugs EDM Series No 12. WHO/EDM/PAR/2002.3

ANNEX 2

Commission on Intellectual Property Rights
Summary of Recommendations Relating to the Patent System:

Developing countries:

*Exclude totally from patentability diagnostic, therapeutic and surgical methods for the treatment of humans and animals
* Exclude from patentability plants and animals and adopt a restrictive definition of microorganisms
* Exclude from patentability computer programmes and business methods
* Avoid patenting of new uses of known products
* Avoid using the patent system to protect plant varieties and where possible, genetic material
* Provide for international exhaustion of patent rights
* Provide and effective compulsory licensing system and adequate government use provisions
* Provide broadest possible exceptions to patent rightsincluding adequate research exemptions exception and an explicit 'Bolar exception'
* Apply strict standards on novelty, inventive step and industrial application or utility (consider higher standards than currently applied in developed countries)
*Make use of strict patentability and disclosure requirements to prevent unduly broad claims in patent applications
* Provide a relatively low cost opposition or re-examination procedure
* Provide means to prevent the granting or enforcement of patents comprising biological material or associated traditional knowledge obtained in contravention of access legislation or the provisions of the CBD
* Consider providing alternative forms of protection to encourage sub-patentable type local innovation

For developed and developing countries

* Apply an absolute standard of novelty such that any disclosure anywhere in the world can be considered prior art
* Take greater account of traditional knowledge when examining patent applications
* Provide the obligatory disclosure of information in the patent application of the geographical source of biological materials from which the invention is derived.

Least developed countries

* Delay providing protection for pharmaceutical products until at least 2016. Those who currently provide protection for such products should seriously consider amending their legislation..

Source: CIPR (2002), *Integrating intellectual property rights and development policy,* Commission on Intellectual Property Rights, London.

IV
INTERNATIONAL NON-STATE ACTORS AND SOCIAL DEVELOPMENT POLICY

Paul Stubbs

Associate Senior Researcher
Globalism and Social Policy Programme (GASPP)
University of Sheffield, UK

1. Introduction: Questions, Definitions, Approach

This paper seeks to discuss the role of international non-state actors in the complex multi-lateralism of social and development policy marked as it is by a high, and sometimes seemingly unfathomable, degree of institutional fragmentation and competition. It focuses on two broad groups of actors, international NGOs (INGOs) and international consultancy companies (ICCs), who are key players in the global politics of aid and development but whose activities are rarely scrutinised with analytical precision and, indeed, rarely studied together. The study builds on earlier GASPP work and, in particular, draws on papers presented at the third GASPP seminar on 'International NGOs, Consulting Companies and Global Social Policy', held in Helsinki in December 1999, as well as a number of subsequent texts linking INGOs, ICCs and Global Social Policy (Deacon 2000; de la Porte and Deacon 2002).

The text is also informed by the author's own work in South-Eastern Europe, both researching international organisations and, increasingly, undertaking consultancy, advice, project and programme design, implementation and evaluation work, some of which has been for INGOs and, indeed, in two instances, for different ICCs. Increasingly, my own research and scientific work has utilised an ethnographic perspective (Stubbs 2002), studying aid relationships, or "how aid happens" (Wedel 2001, 6) within particular societies at particular times. Here, the intention is to 'scale up' the analysis from the micro- to the macro- level, tying specific causes for concern to more general issues raised by a number of commentators in the wider development literature. In the process, I seek to illuminate a series of important policy issues for Finland and like-minded governments as donors in social development contexts. The recommendations at the end of this paper build on existing work and seek to complement recommendations in the other policy briefs in striving to work towards "a rule-based international … system that ensures the social welfare of all the world's citizens" (Deacon 2002).

The key questions being asked here include:

- how can the increasing significance of international non-state aid and development actors, whose motivation must contain a degree of self-interest, be reconciled with the increasing call for value based global social reform?

- has the increasing harnessing of some of these actors to specific donor agendas and frameworks helped or hindered in the development of global social rights?

- are such agencies 'too close for comfort' (Hulme and Edwards 1997) to donors at the expense of constituencies in the developing and transition countries, including Southern NGOs and poor people and their movements?

- is there an inevitable contradiction between competing to deliver aid and development programmes as sub-contractors and being critics and advocates for change in the global social reform agenda?

- what changes are needed, and which are feasible, to ensure a more progressive role for these international non state actors in future social and development policy?

1.1 Definitions

The concepts used in this paper are informed by and, in turn, contribute to, a particular value-theoretical orientation which should be stated very clearly at the outset. Much of this comes from recent attempts to merge social policy analysis with insights from development studies. Thus social policy itself may be defined as "… any policy developed at supranational, state, local or community level which is underpinned by a social vision of society and which, when operationalised, affects the rights or abilities of citizens to meet their livelihood needs. (Overseas Development Administration 1995, 26) " The study of 'global social policy', therefore, is concerned with an analysis of "which supranational and global agencies are actors in the emerging processes of influencing national policy and engaging in transnational *redistribution*, supranational *regulation* and supranational and global *provision*. (Deacon et al 1997, 22) " In essence, this is what is meant in the text by 'social development policy', although, often, indices of official development assistance (ODA), as a particular form of transnational transfer, is taken as a proxy for this, albeit a poor one.

Recent work undertaken by social policy and development studies scholars at the University of Bath, UK, is particularly useful in helping to define the terms of the debate here. In a recent article, Ian Gough (2001) has outlined eight elements of what he terms 'the extended welfare mix', based on Geof Wood's earlier notion of the 'institutional responsibility matrix'. The table below seems to me to be an extraordinarily useful way of extending welfare regime analysis, with its traditional focus on social policy within one country, which sees welfare as produced and allocated in and through the inter-relationships of the state, the market, community and households, to encompass the role of global, supra-national, transnational or international actors alongside that of domestic actors.

TABLE 1: The Extended Welfare Mix[1]

	Domestic	Supra-national
State	1. Domestic governance	5. International org's, national donors
Market	2. Domestic markets	6. Global Markets, MNCs (multi-national corporations)
Community	3. Civil Society, NGOs	7. International NGOs
Household	4. Households	8. International household strategies

The model draws attention to the role of these eight different broad actors in the production of welfare and security, and its converse, insecurity. In addition, it suggests that social policy must be understood in power terms, not as a technical issue, by embedding these actors in the deep structures of social reproduction through a political economy approach. Thirdly, it focuses on the interactions between global pressures and local forces in producing welfare regimes. In addition, I would suggest that it introduces a greater degree of indeterminancy and flexibility in terms of an understanding of why certain policy outcomes develop. Indeed, the mode of analysis which looks at disagreements over policies within as well as between supra-national actors is a particularly important one (Deacon et al 1997).

For our purposes here, the fifth and sixth categories in the matrix, those of Supra-National Markets (Global Markets and MNCs), and Supra-National Community (INGOs), are of greatest interest. These two components could be aggregated as a kind of Global Intermediate Category between the Global Public (IGOs and donors),

---

[1] Gough, Ian *op. Cit.* p. 169; numbers of matrix entries added.

and the Global Household or Global Private (international household strategies). At the global level they are the correlates of those national actors which are neither fully public (as is the state) nor fully private (as is the household).

Having aggregated the two categories there is the need for a new disaggregation which is more like a continuum, with Multi-National Corporations, for profit, at one end, and International or Global Civil Society, not for profit, at the other end. In between are a growing group of Service Contractors, oriented to providing services in international aid and development markets. This group can be discussed as a whole since they, essentially, compete for many of the same contracts, whether or not they are, technically, not-for profit (INGOs) or for-profit (ICCs). Income derived from providing these services, running programmes and projects and so on, is income whether or not a part of it is distributed as a dividend to owners and shareholders. In a sense, it is these 'hybrid' organisations, with a strong market-orientation but also a public purpose, which are the main focus of this study. The notion of Service Contractors derives from David Korten's (1990) earlier notion of Public Service Contractors who "sell their services to aid donors and government agencies to implement projects and programmes" (Robinson 1997, 59).

A similar focus is developed by Kees Biekhart in his pioneering study of democratic transitions in Central America where he refers to 'private aid agencies', although interestingly, he equates these with INGOs or Northern NGOs precisely on the basis of their value orientation, being, he argues "primarily driven by humanitarian values instead of profits ... originating in compassion and altruism" (Biekhart 1999,60). This insistence on focussing exclusively on INGOs rather than ICCs allows Biekhart to examine "how (and why) many private aid agencies committed to social change in the 1990s have shifted away from solidarity aid and appear to have surrendered to a market-driven culture in which solidarity has been replaced by the safer route of simple charity provision" (ibid, 18). Nevertheless, by not referring at all to ICCs, the approach poses some problems for an understanding of the range of actors active in the aid and develement market.

In contrast, Janine Wedel's highly influential study of Western Aid to Eastern Europe in the early 1990s, notes the role of the 'Big Six' Western accountancy firms who "with contracts from USAID, the EU PHARE program, the British Know How Fund, the World Bank, the EBRD, and others, ... began to establish offices in Central and Eastern Europe and to launch commercial activities" (Wedel 2001, 51). The value base of this group differs substantially from those studied by Biekhart, of course, but they are also Service Contractors and, as such, need to be studied as international non-state actors in social development. The fact that Price Waterhouse Coopers, a major accountancy firm, itself formed from the merger of two of the 'Big Six' companies, has recently advertised for a social policy co-ordinator in view of its increasing work in this field, should alert us to the increasing importance, massively under-researched, of this group in global social development policy.

At the other end of the continuum, are solidaristic social movements who do not engage in service activities, 'transnational advocacy networks' (Keck and Sikkink 1998) (who form a kind of, more or less loose and fluid, 'transnational public sphere' (Guidry et al 2000, 5), promoting "models of human rights, consumer rights, environmental regulation, social and economic development, and human equality and justice" (Meyer et al 1997, 165) Interestingly from the perspective of the argument presented here, Duffield's concern that, in the Balkans crisis, solidaristic Western peace and women's groups, also began to become service contractors, receiving donor funds to stimulate particular local constituencies, shows the complexity of the typology and continuum (Duffield 1996). Often in the literature structural forms are confused with questions of motivations and values, as in the idea of a clear-cut three-fold distinction between 'instrumentalist goals', 'shared causal ideas', and 'shared principled ideas or values' (Keck and Sikkink 1998, 30). Certainly, seeing Service-oriented INGOs and ICCs as an intermediate category does not preclude them seeking to maximise their income and/ or engaging in value-led activities, although the legal status of, say the 'trading' and 'campaigning' arms of registered NGOs or non-profits can be complex in certain national contexts.

In a sense, the whole focus has to be historically specific, tracing shifts over time in the development of what might best be termed the **supranational intermediate sphere**. In addition, the typology must be built on a recognition that many important new initiatives in global social governance further erode the 'public/private' dichotomy such as notions of 'corporate social responsibility' and of 'public-private partnerships' which are the subject of other policy briefs in this series and/or ongoing GASPP interest and work. In addition, the definition needs to address the inter-relationships between local and supra-national players. Nevertheless, the rest of this text is based on an expansion of Wood and Gough's matrix to include a new category, that of the intermediate sphere, between the market and the community sphere, albeit with very permeable borders with both[2]. Whilst the emphasis in this text is on group 8, this cannot be undertaken in isolation from interactions with all other parts of the matrix nor, within a broad political economy approach, from changing historical and structural processes and contexts.

---

[2] The supranational intermediate sphere also would include groups such as international professional associations, international churches in their religious function, international political groupings, international trade union groups, and so on. Unless involved explicitly in social development, however, such groups are excluded from consideration in this study.

TABLE 2: The Extended Welfare Mix: the intermediate sphere

	Domestic	*Supra-national*
State	1. Domestic governance	6. International org's, national donors
Market	2. Domestic Markets	7. Global Markets, MNCs
Intermediate	3. National Service NGOs and Consultancy Companies	8. INGOs and ICCs
Community	4. Local Social Movements	9. Global Social Movements
Household	5. Households	10. International household strategies

A related definitional problem concerns exactly what is meant by 'international' when discussing INGOs and ICCs. The literal sense of linking more than one nation could apply to registration, membership, staffing and/or operations. Much of the literature is vague on this point although definitions of INGOs as operating in three or more countries are sometimes taken as the benchmark (Weiss 1999, 5). In addition, because most of the data derive from OECD member states, the notion of 'international' actually becomes a strange and somewhat inadequate synonym for bodies with their origins, membership, and ownership, in 'Western', 'Northern' or developed countries but who work outside these countries. This practice is continued here despite its problems, to distinguish these non-state actors from emerging non-state actors with their origins in the developing and transitional worlds which may also be 'international'. Obviously, the relation between these two sets of actors is, itself, complex and changing.

1.2 The Argument

This text seeks to build on this definitional foundation by examining, in broad terms, the historical lineages of international non-state actors (section 2). It then goes on to try to assess their income and to address certain trends within the sector (Section 3). The core of the text focuses on the role of international non-state actors within what is described as an emerging New International Aid and Development Regime (Section 4). Elements of this are discussed through two European case studies (Section 5). The text ends with a series of broad recommendations for Finland and like minded countries (Section 6).

Crucially, the context of increasing poverty and inequalities within and between countries, regions and across the globe as a whole, in part related to particular kinds of global inclusions and exclusions, is the stark reality against which this and other policy briefs are written. The role of international non-state actors in influencing and affecting 'the state of the world's welfare' is too important and too complex to be addressed by simple formulas, whether these are moralistic condemnations of the inevitable co-option of the 'Lords of Poverty', or a faith in new technical measures which will, finally, make a big difference. The need for a new architecture of global social governance which is being advocated in all these policy papers will still involve a significant, if changed, role for international non-state actors.

2. International Non-State Actors in Historical Perspective

2.1 International Non-State Actors and the World Polity

In seeking to understand the contemporary and, indeed, future, role of international non-state actors, it is important to adopt a very long term historical perspective. Boli and Thomas trace their origins to the emergence of a 'contemporary world polity', "rooted in Christendom and Western law ..., the Enlightenment ..., and, at least through the nineteenth century, the Roman Catholic church..." (Boli and Thomas 1999, 305). The growth and integration of the world economy, European imperialism, and the development of global transportation and communication systems, also in the nineteenth century, which elsewhere they describe as a complex mixture of "colonization, economic expansion, and evangelization" (ibid, 303) should be seen as the key underpinnings of the sector.

The origins are, therefore, certainly, Northern and Western, but also complex and contradictory. Whilst it is important to recognise "the decisive importance of scientific knowledge in sustaining and guiding technological development after 1850" (Castells 1996, 34), in which older professions such as accountancy, the forebearers of emerging ICCs, helped to forge a new rationality, this is not the whole story. Religious thought continued to be of importance. In addition, it is certainly true that, from the very beginning, elements of the non-governmental charity sector developed 'anti-core agendas' (ibid), notably the British and Foreign Anti-Slavery Society, founded in 1839[3]. In fact, adding militarism to the equation, so that the sector has, indeed, always been based on the complex inter-relationship between imperialistic militarism, religious evangelism, scientific rationalism, and political oppositionalism, helps to place debates about development and humanitarianism in their proper context.

---

[3] The organisation still exists today, and is now known as Anti-Slavery International (cf. Chabbott, Colette 1999, 228.)

Boli and Thomas analyse data on 5,983 INGOs founded between 1875 and 1988 and listed in the Yearbook of International Organisations which has been published since 1950 by the Union of International Organisations. This body traces its origins to the Central Office of International Organisations, founded in Brussels in 1907 and actively involved in the founding of the League of Nations (Boli and Thomas 1999, 20 ff., 305) As an overview of the wider INGO sector the study is unsurpassed in the literature, although it is only complete until 1973. A number of important themes emerge, including:

- Trends in the founding of INGOs match the 'general state of the world', with steady growth until World War 1 and then a steep decline; faster growth until World War 2 followed by another steep decline; and then an 'explosion' of growth after World War 2, maintained until 1973. Indeed, although much fewer in number, the trend is remarkably consistent with that of the founding of Inter-Governmental Organisations (IGOs).

- Organisations with a regional focus, which "limit their membership by territorial or ascriptive criteria" (ibid, 30), were rare until after World War 2, but have expanded greatly since, with more regional than global bodies founded for the first time in 1959. Regional NGOs were, at first, predominantly European, then increasing numbers were founded in the Americas, and, from the 1960s, in Asia and Africa.

- Nearly 60% of all INGOs concentrate on economic, scientific and technical issues, representing a core of 'peculiarly invisible' organisations. Those described as 'Individual Rights/Welfare', and 'World-polity' INGOs, including many of the most prominent INGOs, rights-based organisations, relief and charity organisations, and environmental groups, account for only 14% of the total (ibid, 42-43).

There is no equivalent study, to my knowledge, of International Consultancy Companies, although their origins must also lie in the alliance of rational science, expert systems and professional services which achieved a relative autonomy from, and an indispensability for, emerging transnational trade, particularly in the nineteenth century. KPMG, one of the leading International Consultancy Companies, for example, traces its origins back to national firms established in the UK in 1870 and in the USA in 1897, merging to become Peat Marwick International (PMI) a worldwide network of accountancy and consultancy companies, as early as 1911 (www.kpmg.com). A major boost to the sector came with the rise in the West, from the 1970s, of what

Castells has termed the 'service economy' including productive, distributive, personal (leisure) and, interestingly, social services (Castells 1996, 209-216). Hence, within a new international division of labour, the conditions for the increasing importance of Western knowledge-based service systems in global markets were created.

Subsequently, it is the revolution in information technology in the last decade, and its massive impact on the nature of 'work', which provides the conditions for an explosion of International Consultancy, not just by companies but by an emerging army of free-lance consultants able to sell intellectual services in real and virtual space, either directly to clients or through mediating agents, companies or institutions. Again, Castells' insights are pivotal here, arguing that the 'emerging informational paradigm' introduces a new division of labour based on values, relationships and decisions which opens up a new space for a class of flexi-workers able to innovate and integrate through participation in and control of knowledge and information networks (ibid, 243-4). It is this new flexible space into which consultancy work fits as a hand into a glove.

The rise of a new non-permanent Western professional labour force consists of professionals who supplement their regular work with consultancies; senior professionals and executives who have retired (sometimes early); those in academia and similar bodies whose positions and/or promotions require the raising of external revenue through providing services; and a more transient and complex group, particularly those with existing experience with a range of international organisations, civil, military, public and private. It is what Castells terms the 'individualization' or, perhaps better, the 'detraditionalization' of labour which is crucial here, allowing for both a decentralisation of work tasks and their re-co-ordination in real time through a virtual interactive network of communication. The growth of "subcontracting, outsourcing, offshoring, **consulting**, downsizing, and customizing" (ibid, 265 *emphasis added*) thus becomes of immense importance. Whilst this began as a phenomenon in the North and the West, the extent of the incorporation of the East and the South into this is an area worthy of more exploration.

2.2 International Development Organisations

The Origins of Development INGOs

As a sub-set of INGOs, a group of organisations emerged in high-income countries to promote 'development' in low-income countries of Latin America, Asia and Africa and, later, in 'transition' countries of Central and Eastern Europe and the former Soviet Union. Of 1,620 INGOs studied by Chabott, about one third (532) confine their activities to development advocacy, or education of the public in high-income countries. The remaining 1,088 are actively engaged in operational development activities, providing "funds, personnel and materials for actions undertaken in low-income countries" (Chabbot 1999, 227). Of these development INGOs, over 80% were founded in the post-war period, i.e. from 1946 – 1985, concurrent with the emergence of modern concepts of 'international development'.

The organisations founded before this are of particular interest. Chabbott suggests that those founded before World War 1 fall into three groups: missionary organisations; specialised humanitarian organisations (most notably the International Committee of the Red Cross founded in 1863); and professional, labour and political solidarity groups. Particularly interesting is the fact that "over two thirds of the development INGOs with founding dates prior to 1900 and surviving until the early 1990s mention a religion explicitly in their titles" (ibid, 228). Chabbott traces, also, three types of development INGOs emerging in the period between the two World Wars. The first of these are private philanthropies, although the Carnegie and Rockefeller Foundations were actually founded just before World War 1, and the Ford Foundation, although founded in 1936, was not particularly active until the late 1940s. The second group was specialised sectoral organisations, particularly focused on health and population issues. The third group were emergency relief organisations such as the Committee for the Relief of Belgium, established in 1914, and Save the Children, UK founded in 1919. Another surge in the founding of development INGOs occurred during World War 2 with a number of groups founded which would later become some of the biggest development INGOs, such as Oxfam, Catholic Relief Services, CARE, and Lutheran World Relief.

Growth

The period from 1945 to 1970 can be seen to have been the pre-cursor for the later 'explosion' of development actors, or what has been termed the 'golden era' of private foreign aid (Biekhart 1999, 68). The underpinnings of this can be traced to a number of wider, chronologically overlapping, contextual factors. These include:

1. The creation of the United Nations and its agencies from 1946 onwards, key to the 'new humanitarianism' (Black 1986), spawning new UN support associations, and itself engaging in global redistribution and provision as well as regulation.

2. The emerging role of the United States, during the Cold War, as a bilateral development actor, often using aid funds to pursue wider foreign policy objectives, with many US war relief agencies adapting to work closely with the US government and, from the 1950s, playing a key role in food aid programmes (Biekhart 1999, 66).

3. The creation of special Ministries or Offices for Development Co-Operation in the early 1960s[4], following the formation of the Development Assistance Committee (DAC) of the OECD, all of which began to devote funds to international non-state actors and, more importantly, to provide a greater legitimacy for 'development' as a public discourse in the developed world.

4. The conjunction of radicalism and decolonization in the 1960s, stimulating new thinking about aid and development and leading to the establishment of new Northern organisations and networks and the radicalisation of others (notably some church groups), with a much greater emphasis on social change and the need to switch from relief of poverty to a focus on the underlying structural causes of poverty.

Biekhart traces four factors associated with the 'golden age' for European and Canadian non-state development actors in the 1970s and 1980s: a massive increase in funding, mainly from official sources; a more pronounced domestic profile, aided by the revolution in communications; a polarised global climate; and the massive growth of Southern NGOs and social movements. Taken together, these provided a clear space for non-state actors to work as intermediaries in development contexts, as a potential 'countervailing power' constructing 'chains of solidarity' (Biekhart 1999, 73). His concept of an increasing divergence between US and non-US actors is important, linked to the emergence of the World Bank as a major, some would argue *the* major, development actor in the 1980s, perhaps not coincidentally staffed proportionately by many more US citizens than the UN agencies (Chabbott 1999, 247).

Crisis

The role of the World Bank, the United States and, to an extent, the United Kingdom and others, in the promotion of a 'neo-liberal' policy agenda replacing, at least in part, that of a social democratic agenda, both at home and abroad, seemed, at first sight, to be an opportunity for INGOs active in international development. After all, the promotion of the view that "markets and private initiative are ... the most efficient mechanisms for achieving economic growth and providing most services to most people" (Hulme and Edwards 1997, 5) and, even more so, the vital importance given

---

[4] Biekhart (1999, 67) "Special ministries to administer development aid were created in France, Germany and Switzerland in 1961; Belgium, Denmark and Sweden in 1962; the Netherlands in 1963; Great Britain in 1964; and Canada in 1968." (ff. p. 309).

to Non-Governmental, grassroots and civil society organisations in development, created conditions for increased funding in the short term at least.

This was, however, very much a double-edged sword since the professional staff of many of these NGOs, and the core of supporters 'back home' were not ideologically pre-disposed to the new policy orthodoxy. In a sense a new 'identity crisis' developed, in which the divergence between US and European agencies increased, and became more ideological. Perhaps even more importantly, a group of INGOs in the middle grappled much more than ever before with the contradiction between their broad motivation for social change and social justice and the organisational requirements of securing a lucrative aid contract, or what Michael Edwards termed the tension between 'developmental' and 'institutional imperatives' (Biekhart 1999, 77). Some managed the contradiction better than others, using a proportion of aid contract funds to cover the costs of research and policy departments which became the 'value added' contribution of INGOs in terms of development policy debates.

In any case, as Biekhart reminds us, income for INGOs began to stagnate in the 1990s, as general ODA stagnated (these trends are explored more in Section 3 below). The public development discourse began to exhibit increased doubts about, and hence concern with, efficiency and effectiveness, fuelled by official reports and popular exposees which demonstrated INGOs' poor performance, lack of accountability, and financial profligacy. Southern NGOs became increasingly important, often being preferred by donors as more efficient and effective partners, and themselves critiquing the neo-colonialism and interference which Northern and Western INGOs brought to the aid relationship. Indeed, the complex merging of neo-liberal economics with grassroots emphases on 'participation' and 'sustainable development' further eroded the space for Western INGOs to continue as before.

The identity crisis was profound and, in a sense, is still continuing. Many have commented on the 'weak learning' patterns of INGOs which have "contributed to a basic lack of clarity about future form and function and has manifested itself in an unprecedented period of self-questioning, with almost continuous strategic revisions, restructurings and new mission statements" (Madon 2000). Biekhart's (1999, 74) conclusion that, in the 1990s, "it was now a matter of institutional survival to behave as 'for profits' in a non-profit environment" represents one way out of this, as many INGOs pursued a much more instrumentalist path than previously. At this point, some of the research and policy development departments noted above lost ground to, or transformed into, public relations departments concerned much more with 'marketing', even 'branding', INGOs (Ritchie et al 1999)

This fundamental reorganisation of many leading INGOs, introducing 'modern methods' evolved by 'management consultants' in the private sector (with the texts of management gurus like Tom Peters replacing those of earlier favoured authors such as

Paolo Friere and Saul Alinsky (Hulme and Edwards 1997, 280), itself led to points of joint interest and approach with a new generation of emerging development ICCs. In any case, the massive increase in funds to respond to complex humanitarian emergencies from the mid-1980s, also fuelled short-termism, projectisation, and intense competition within the aid market, and detracted from wider development thinking and action.

Unlike Western INGOs, International Development Consultancy Companies have gone from strength to strength, and become increasingly important in this environment. This can be linked to the broad upsurge in conditions for consultancy noted above, as well as the specifics of the emerging aid market noted below. Above all, the increasing emphasis on particular business principles in aid and development, creates a niche for a range of development consultancy companies, some of which have this aspect as a new or expanding arm of their work, and others of which are newly formed. What is less clear is whether the trend has yet spread, in any large extent, to the South, although the erosion of critical research and analytic capacity through short-term consultancy has been remarked upon by one influential commentator (Mkandawire 1998).

In a sense, the focus needs to be as much on the core personnel, often exhibiting 'revolving door' tendencies, moving between different types of agencies as well as increasingly engaged as consultants, and on their motivations and profiles, rather than exclusively on organisational forms. Some have suggested that there has been a narrowing and not a broadening of the profiles, skills, motivations, and career paths of professionals in development, with increasing specialisation in technical issues. This is relevant for our discussion, below, of the new aid and development regime.

However, this is not the whole story. The informational revolution has allowed for a mushrooming of policy institutes, think-tanks, and flexible advice agencies with a much more critical stance towards the orthodoxies of development and the stance of major IGOs and donor agencies[5]. Many of these combine monitoring, advocacy and advice-giving with a broader political orientation and a keen desire to search for alternatives. Critical development studies scholars also offer alternative positions and programmes, seemingly not unduly co-opted by their increasing involvement in consultancy. Donors themselves are increasingly interested in funding initiatives which offer a longer-term perspective on social change from within developing countries. Nevertheless, the issue of the significance of the international non-state sector must be addressed continuously if there is to be an opportunity for real learning in social development contexts.

---

[5] The Bretton Woods Project, set up in 1995 to support a network of UK NGOs, with considerable influence on policy debates regarding the reform of the World Bank and the IMF, is one example.

3. Size Matters: Baselines and Trends

3.1 A New Baseline?

Notwithstanding the increasing focus on technicisation, efficiency and value for money within development projects, it was only in the year 2000 that a new baseline for assessing the financial size of development NGOs emerged. Even then, "the first systematic and empirical profile of a sector that has, to date, proved factually elusive" (Woods 2000, 33), only covers European development NGOs and not those with their seats in the United States, Canada, Japan, Australia or New Zealand. Utilising, for the first time, NGOs' own reports of their income rather than donor's reports, the study analyses responses from 1,832 European development NGOs who provided detailed information on their budgets (only 41% of all those in the original OECD (1996) database). This showed that the total income of these INGOs for 1993 was 7.3 billion USD. This is itself approximately equal to what had been assumed previously to be the total figure for development NGOs in *all* OECD countries. The study acknowledges the possibility of some double counting but suggests that if, at a conservative estimate, this is taken to be the total income for all European NGOs then the OECD figure for 1993 is some 15.5 billion USD, or 28% of the then total ODA of OECD member states.

The study divides the sources of this income into three: Official Sources (from governments and multi-lateral agencies) which accounts for 42% of all income of those surveyed; Private Sources (essentially voluntary donations) which also accounts for 42%; and Self-Financing (through trading and consultancy services) accounting for 16%[6]. In addition, the study shows a very high degree of income concentration and inequality within the sector, with the top 20% of NGOs accounting for 90.5% of total income, the middle 60% accounting for 9%, and the bottom 20% accounting for less than 0.5%[7]. The top 10 income earners (only 0.55% of those reporting) account for 21% of the sector's income (a total of 1.533 billion USD with Italian Caritas in first place with reported funds of 275 m USD, with others in the top 10 including Save the Children UK with 130 m. USD and OXFAM UK with 118 m. USD[8]). The 1,983

---

[6] Ibid, p. 18. The figures for NGOs based in Finland are Official Sources 32%; Private Sources 41%; and Self-Financing 20%, ibid. p. 19.

[7] Ibid. p19, The figures for Finland are: top 20% - 85.5%; middle 60% - 14%; bottom 20% - <0.5%, ibid. p. 20.

[8] Some of these figures are very similar to those provided for the same period, compiled from a variety of sources, by Kees Biekhart, *op. cit.* p. 61. Some of those not in the top ten in the OECD study, are of immense importance not least because of their high reliance on official aid, notably the German EZE (fifth in Biekhart's list with a 1993 income of 117.8 m. USD, 90% of which was from official sources, and the Danish Refugee Council (sixth in Biekhart's list with income of 105.6 m. USD, 98% from official sources).

NGOs who provided data on staff and volunteers reported employing a total of 86,344 salaried staff, with almost ten times as many volunteers. UK NGOs accounted for almost one quarter of all salaried staff (21,227), 67% of whom were working in developing countries as compared with 45% for the sample as a whole[9].

The publication of such a study in 2000, based on figures for 1993, is itself symptomatic of a chronic lack of factual data. The study, as its author records, "certainly serves to challenge the adequacy of existing methods of statistical reporting on NGOs" (OECD 1996, 33). The massive underestimation of the extent of official funding for NGOs which the study appears to have revealed, largely a result of previous reliance on donor figures which often do not include bilateral funds and emergency funds, both of which have actually increased in importance since 1993, is particularly worrying in terms of any attempt to hold an informed debate on the extent to which international development NGOs have become 'too close for comfort' to official donors.

There is no equivalent, easily accessible, data on the income of International Development Consultancy Companies, at least to my knowledge. The increasing importance of the sector can be gauged, however, from an analysis of "100 leading international development firms, NGOs, and agencies" compiled and sold, in return for sharing the purchasers' cv with all 100, by Developmentex.com as "a critical tool for to begin researching, networking, and working hard towards that international development job you're dreaming of" (www.developmentex.com). Two thirds of those listed are consultancy firms, with the remainder INGOs, academic institutes or their off-shoots, with a very small number whose exact status is unclear from the description and web-page. Very few list their annual income although those which do include Abt Associates (US-based, founded in 1965) with an income of 184 m USD, only a fraction of which is for development work. Crown Agents, a UK company which was part of the public sector until privatised in 1997, states that, in joint ventures, it is involved in contracts totalling 6 billion GBP (about 9 billion USD).

Far more typical are the following three ICCs:

- Creative Associates International is "a Washington-based private consulting firm specialising in community development and post-conflict assistance; educational development and communication and technology application for development" (ibid), founded in 1997, it has over 200 staff, 12 field offices, and estimates

---

[9] The figures for Finnish NGOs differ substantially from the average. Of 2,497 salaried personnel, 85% work in Europe, the 7th highest figure of 22 countries. Of 36,764 volunteers, 27% are based in developing countries, which is 6th highest, ibid. pp. 23-24.

2001 revenue at 35 m. USD with over 200 m. USD worth of work in signed contracts.

- GOPA-Consultants is a large international development consultancy based in Germany, specializing in human resources development with a Department for Human Resources and Social Development which "realises the vital importance of adequate social security and social services coverage for social peace and political and economic stability" (www.gopa.de). Founded in 1963, it had 189 staff in 2001 and turnover of approximately 34 m USD.
- Cowater describes itself as one of Canada's largest development consultancy firms concentrating on water and sanitation; financial management, audit and accounting; and social development. Its Social Development Group focuses "on activities designed to improve the well-being of individuals and communities; community development and mobilization; gender impact analysis; social communication; institutional analysis and assessment; processes that promote participation in decisions that affect people's lives; socio-economic assessments; and identification and inclusion of women's needs and priorities, as well as those of vulnerable and disadvantaged groups" (www.cowater.com). Founded in 1985, Cowater's annual consolidated revenue exceeds 10 m $ CAN or 6.35 m. USD.

This suggests that the proportion of development income going to consultancy companies, whilst less than to INGOs, is not insignificant. It also shows that, in fact, one of the most important tasks of these firms is to hold cv's which are important commodities in terms of a new flexible consultancy system – one firm boasts that it has over 6000 cv's on file. The need for more research on development consultancy companies, including studies of their practices on the ground, is a major issue which is only just beginning to be addressed in the literature on global social policy (See Box 5.1 below).

3.2 Discerning Trends

Given the new baseline from the OECD European NGO study, and the absence of a baseline for consultancy companies, trends over time are increasingly hard to discern. If we make some assumptions that trends reported in the development literature are true, at least in relative terms, whilst underestimating real income for INGOs, then the following observations are important, at least for the period until the mid-1990s:

- In the context of declining or stagnant ODA[10], the proportion dispersed through INGOs and, we may infer, through ICCs, increased dramatically, in part through the increasing importance of emergency aid[11], and in part because of a wider agenda of sub-contracting, both bilaterally and multi-laterally. ECHO, the European Commission's Humanitarian Office, for example, channelled between a half and two thirds of its funding through NGOs in the first five years of the 1990s[12].

- Within the INGO sector, there has been increasing internationalisation and oligopolisation with eight 'super NGOs', actually families or federations of INGOs (including CARE International, Oxfam International, World Vision International, Save the Children Alliance, Caritas International) perhaps having half of all aid income dispersed through NGOs (Donini 1996), and as much as 80% of the financial value of assistance in complex emergencies" (Gordenker and Weiss 1996, 218) by 1995.

- In the early 1990s there was a 'mushrooming' or perhaps resurgence is a better term, of 'democracy assistance', led by the United States and oriented particulary to countries in transition in Central and Eastern Europe and the former Soviet Union[13]. This trend was amplified by the European Union concerned, ultimately, with accession in some of the same countries and, more specifically, by German government support for former Eastern Germany (Burnell 2000, 49). This tended to promote packages of technical assistance which empowered a new generation of INGOs and, in particular, consultancy companies and individual consultants, and led to a global emphasis on 'governance' and 'civil society' as crucial elements of social development.

---

[10] It is widely accepted that ODA declined between 1991 and 1997, although 1995 saw a relative increase. UNRISD (2000) *Visible Hands: taking responsibility for social development* Geneva: UNRISD, p. 27 charts a 4.6% decline in real terms.

[11] Bosnia, Rwanda, Kosov, and East Timor became watchwords for new international crises with hundreds of INGOs appearing to descend overnight.

12 Weiss, Thomas (1999) 'International NGOs, Global Governance, and Social Policy in the UN System, *GASPP Occasional Papers* 3; p. 14. Whilst much of this may be attributable to the wars of the Yugoslav succession, Weiss' wider point that the EU itself channeled 95% of aid directly to Governments in 1976 but only 6% in 1990, and correspondingly aid through NGOs went from zero to 37% in the same period.

[13] Carothers, Thomas (1999) *Aiding Democracy Abroad: the learning curve* Washington DC: Carnegie Endowment for International Peace. "(O)ver the course of the 1990s the U.S. Government spent close to $ 1 billion on democracy programs for the post-Communist countries of Eastern Europe and the former Soviet Union", ibid. p. 41.

- The role of USAID, the World Bank and the European Union as aid donors and lenders linking grants and credits with technical assistance has fuelled the growth of consultancies through competitive tendering. This has led to an increasing emphasis within the sector on the development of programme consortia bringing a range of expertise to their work. In addition, the formal or informal 'tying' of personnel, in which consultants from EU member states or from the US are appointed to positions which represent a significant proportion of aid for a particular programme, has become increasingly common. At the same time, many donor agencies have out-sourced some of what were, previously, their core functions to consultants, including reviews, policy advice and speech writing. Sometimes these are bundled together within framework consultancies whereby, on the basis of competitive tendering, one firm handles all requests for advice and assistance up to an agreed financial limit.

- There has been an emergence of what might best be termed 'supra-philanthropy' with the establishment of new private foundations by particularly successful business leaders which make interventions in aid and development which are relatively large and which are tied to specific aims and objectives. George Soros' Open Society Fund was the first of these, of course, originally focused on emerging democracies in Central and Eastern Europe and the former Soviet Union. The initiatives by Ted Turner (Turner Foundation) and Bill Gates (the Bill and Melinda Gates Foundation) are also relevant, with the latter, focused on health, also providing a stimulus for international non-state actors.

Taken together, these issues point to the need to look in greater detail at the emerging aid and development regime, which is inadequately understood only in terms of statistics and broad trends.

4. The New Aid and Development Regime: contrasts and continuities

4.1 A New Regime?

Since the beginnings of development studies as an academic discipline, every decade has been seen to have ushered in a policy agenda, approach, framework, or discourse which is sufficiently different from the previous one to be described as 'new'. This is greeted skeptically by some old hands who argue, rather, that trends in development are more cyclical or pendulum-like, swinging to and from between competing poles, with little reference to consolidation or lesson learning. Certainly, over time, new themes emerge but rarely replace entirely older themes. When they resemble these older themes, they are never quite the same thing, either, given vastly changed contexts. Over time, this can seem as if development is just becoming more post-modern, complicated, and diverse, with a baffling proliferation of actors, agencies, and forms. An alternative position, beloved of radical critics, is that every new initiative is just the latest trick to consolidate existing power relations.

In this section, we explore elements of what appears to be an emerging aid and development agenda which, for all its complexity, could be developing into a specific 'regime' in the sense of "a set of rules, institutions and structured interests" (Gough 2002). This emerging regime, focused, I would suggest, on **co-ordinated poverty reduction**, has a number of positive and negative features, many of which are familiar and aired frequently in the literature. What is rarely discussed, however, are the implications of the emerging regime for international non-state actors.

At one level, the notion of 'co-ordinated poverty reduction' has always been at the forefront of development assistance. In the 1950s and 1960s, a 'modernization through economic growth' thesis, led by the US on one side and the Soviet bloc on the other, tended to assume that transfers of technology and science would integrate poor countries into a broad economic system, the effects of which would 'trickle down' to their own poor. In the 1970s, there was much greater emphasis on 'equitable growth' and the need to combine a micro-level basic human needs approach (BHN) with a New International Economic Order (NIEO). This was the heyday of the link, in fact, between the UN social agencies' concerns with human development and quality of life, and radicalised and radicalising European INGOs' focus on community development.

The 1980s were dominated by structural adjustment and a privatisation and safety net agenda, with the 1990s much more complex in terms of a resurgence of social concerns, allied with the importance of participatory methods and approaches (Chabbot 1999, 239; *see also* Cooke and Kothari 2001), creating ever more complex and complicated 'aid chains'(Biekhart 1999, 98; Stubbs 2000, 25). The continued decline of the UN agencies, at least operationally, was matched by their increasing importance as arenas for debate, with the Rio, Beijing and Copenhagen summits and, as will be discussed later, in a move towards strategic global development goals. In addition, the World Bank and, later, the IMF changed both in the participatory nature of their approach and, to an extent at least, adapted and diversified their policy prescriptions (Scholte 1998). Some of the effects of this are hotly contested, not least in terms of the suggestion that the World Bank "has adopted and adapted the language of popular participation, rendering it amenable to its own structure and mandate" (Nelson 2000, 149). In addition, ground was certainly lost, from a social rights perspective, as trade agencies, notably the WTO, became increasingly important in the field of global regulation (Koivusalo 1999).

Increasingly, in the 1990s 'programmes' became replaced by 'projects' to such an extent that some authors referred to 'projectisation' as projects proliferated which had, often though not always, meaningful internal aims and objectives but no clear idea of how these fitted into a wider agenda or context. The evidence that international non-state actors did interesting things but, rarely, with the poorest of the poor and, even more rarely, in a way which connected to sustainable policy change, led to a renewed interest in programmes not projects within development agencies. A new coherence, at least in terms of the overall goal, was combined with "a profusion of providers operating in a complex terrain of welfare pluralism" (Lucas and Cornwall 2000).

4.2 Guidelines on Poverty Reduction

The initial parameters of the new approach originated in 1996 with the OECD/DAC strategy paper 'Shaping the 21st Century: the contribution of development co-operation' amplified in the 'DAC Guidelines on Poverty Reduction' published in 2001. In setting out "a vision of development co-operation based on partnerships around development strategies owned and led by developing country governments and civil societies", the focus is on achieving the 'explicit, quantifiable and time-bound' International Development Goals (IDGs) for 2015, endorsed at the UN Millenium Summit in 2001. The document heralds a linguistic shift towards 'partnership' so that 'aid donors' ('the bilateral assistance community') become 'development agencies' and 'recipients' become 'partner countries' or 'partner Governments' with 'developing country civil societies' now 'stakeholders'(OECD 2001, 21).

The approach is based on a strategic framework for translating development goals, through long-term partnerships, into policy actions, based on combining six core policy elements: 'Pro-poor economic growth; Empowerment, rights and pro-poor governance; Basic social services for human development; Human security reducing vulnerability and managing shocks; Mainstreaming of gender and enhancing gender equality; and Mainstreaming environmental sustainability approaches'(ibid, 32). These actions tackle causal factors and can be judged in terms of a series of 'outcome indicators' (ibid, 40-41). The framework seeks explicitly for improved policy co-ordination, consistency and coherence, providing as an Annex an 'Illustrative Checklist on Policy Coherence for Poverty Reduction' which focuses on the inter-connections between foreign, trade and development policies; on co-ordination between bilateral, multi-lateral and global development agencies; and on the internal reform of development agencies themselves and the skills and competences of their staff.

From a global social reformist position, the relative lack of emphasis within the approach on broad social policies, and on social rights, is problematic. It reinforces a tendency, within the IDG approach, to foreclose discussion of wider social policies and of current, and posible future, universal social provision in developing countries. Throughout, 'basic social services' are referred to as synonymous with basic education and health services. In the extended list of major policy issues, social issues is one of seven noted, including only 'Education and training; Social Safety Nets; Public Health systems; Migration; and Public health issues like tropical diseases and tobacco.' In other words, the limited nature of the goals certainly "leaves ample scope for the privatisation of the rest of social provision while international attention is focused only on basic service delivery. (Deacon 2000b, 37)" Similarly, an emphasis on 'Social Investment Funds' (Cornwall and Gaventa 2000, 56), whilst seeking to ensure that lender and donor funding is more responsive to demands from the poor, has actually tended to be implemented by non-state actors, including INGOs and ICCs, thus undermining public provision both in terms of structure and delivery.

The report is also a little reticent about Poverty Reduction Strategy Papers (PRSPs), seeing these as one of a number of "planning frameworks promoted by the international community" as tools to help translate IDGs into national poverty reduction policies, which, in fact, need to be "rationalised to reduce the burden of having partner countries comply with multiple planning instruments" (OECD. PRSPs, approved by the Boards of the World Bank and the International Monetary Fund in December 1999, also purport to focus on promoting 'country-owned poverty reduction strategies' to implement the IDGs, although an enthusiastic internal review of initial work states that "some donors feel that the PRSP process has been dominated by the Bank and the Fund" (Staffs of the World Bank and International Monetary Fund 2002). Whilst there has been a cautious welcome of PRSPs generally, some are beginning to question whether they are "the new face of structural adjustment" (Marshal et al 2001), with an over-emphasis on macro-economic concerns at the expense of an holistic approach.

4.3 Non-State Actors in the New Paradigm

For our concerns here, the relative absence of attention to the role of international non-state actors in the new paradigm is particularly interesting. Much of the thinking within the OECD/DAC paper, including the critique of the 'serious limitations' of 'free-standing projects' outside of national planning frameworks, which has led to an increasing emphasis on sector-wide approaches (SWAps), clearly derives from elements of the critique of the role of INGOs. Whilst there is a focus on 'national civil society' within the approach, and a widening sense of what partners might be, the silence regarding INGOs and ICCs is deafening.

In a sense, one implication of the new approach might be that bilateral development agencies themselves play a much greater role. It may simply be that the focus is so much on this internal change process that the implications for change in relationships with external partners, including INGOs and ICCs, has not been addressed sufficiently thus far. Certainly, if agencies combine decentralisation of their functions with greater co-ordination, then we may see an expansion of their staffing, as has already happened, at least in terms of social development staff, in some bilaterals. The key questions which remain unanswered, at this stage, are how, how far, and in what way, will this new regime affect sub-contracting and other relationships with international non-state actors.

A number of scenarios could occur. The most likely, at least in the short term, is the emergence of a new group of 'poverty reduction strategy' advisors able to translate policy pronouncements into programmes, to evaluate them, and to render them meaningful to a range of agencies in the system. More seriously, the shift from projects to programmes could reinforce tendencies towards concentration, oligopolisation, mergers and consortia amongst non-state actors, since it will be these emerging supranational agencies and alliances who will be the only ones with sufficient capacity to engage in the more complex and coherent programming being developed and likely to increase in importance in the future. Whether this will result in a real increase in programmatic capacity is a more open question, however. It also begs the question of the role of local actors and organisations within emerging consortia. If it is the case that few Southern NGOs or groupings have sufficient capacity to lead the process, might they, once again, become locked into relations of dominance and subordination within a newly revitalised Western development apparatus?

Another option would be that INGOs, in particular, revert to a role which is less focused on operations but, instead reflects "a greater emphasis on monitoring and as a channel of information" between diverse actors, as well as having "a greater role to play in building the capacity of national NGOs to do their own advocacy work and to engage with policy makers to translate grassroots experience into policy" (Woods 2000, 60) This begs a number of questions, including where such INGOs would obtain funding for this work and what space, within the new regime, there is for continued focus on grassroots work and, therefore, its scaling up into policy levels. In addition, there have always been tensions between the wider 'social' focus which some of the more critical INGOs maintain at the global level, and the relative lack of a social policy focus within particular national contexts. In part, this is a product of a development orthodoxy which tends to distrust social policy as a Northern and Western discourse, leaving little space for the articulation of support for public welfare.

4.4 Development and the 'New' Public Management

A wider concern is that the emerging regime is itself a product of the orthodoxy of 'new public management' which applied management concepts originating in the for-profit sector to Western welfare states and, later, to development contexts, as a key element of their 'marketization'. The tenets of the approach have certainly infused development agencies, INGOs and ICCs, including "a sharper focus on (most often quantifiable) results or outcomes …(and) an elevation in cost-management and (economic) efficiency enhancement in the use of public resources" (Ramia *forthcoming*). An approach which shifted the 'social division of welfare' in developed countries, may have unforeseen consequences when it is translated uncritically into development contexts. Most importantly, the effects of the application of a key component of the new public management, 'competitive tendering and contracting', need to be addressed. Proposing such a fundamental shift towards poverty reduction programmes, whilst leaving untouched a 'marketised' sub-contracting regime, does look a little too much like seeking to use 'the master's tools' to dismantle 'the master's house'. The need for regulatory frameworks is recognised within the new orthodoxy, of course: indeed, the shift from a 'providing' state to a 'regulatory' state is, in some ways, at the heart of the new public management. However, there are real problems in the emerging role of international non-state actors in the sphere, akin to a kind of de-regulated regulation.

Whilst a 'market-driven aid system' has certainly been created, markets are of various types and contain imperfections. They need to be studied more closely than they have been thus far. At one level, there may be 'new entrants' to the aid and development market. These might include, in a dominant position, private sector companies, new consultancy firms, and individual consultants from the private sector. The new entrants may, however, be far more diverse than ever before, and include a new group of early-retiree international consultants who are more oriented to traditional Western notions of 'public service', more Southern activists and scholars; new generations of transnational volunteers; and so on.

Another isssue may be the tension between the formal, and ever more complex and tight, rules of contracting and sub-contracting regimes and the continued existence of informal personal and friendship networks amongst the global professional development community. Whilst contracts are rarely awarded on the basis of knowing someone, access to knowledge about contracts may create an imperfection in the market. Increasing specialisation may, again, lead to contracts based on the ability to write good proposals rather than a track record of implementation. In a wider sense, the degree of 'price fixing' within the market, with some leading ICCs able to charge consultants out at rates up to 1500 USD per day, also presents a cause for concern, as does the 'differential pricing' of foreign and local consultants. In any case, such markets are not easily entered by poor people, welfare users, or even by their networks and organisations.

Overall, then, the embracing of the new aid and development agenda by development agencies has unclear implications for the role of international non-state actors in the future. It may well introduce more complex and diverse markets, discourses and organisational forms which will require new kinds of standards, regulations, and frameworks to ensure a balance between innovation and quality control; incorporation and critique; and flexibility and coherence. Unless the role of these international non-state actors is grasped, however, it could prove to be a major Achille's heel of the entire framework.

Some recent thinking on 'output-based aid' (Brook and Smith 2002) seems to be an explicit attempt to apply leassons from the new public management in advanced welfare states to development contexts. At one level, within the global development targets, there is a recognition that anti-poverty strategies must be based on access to good, reliable, public services. However, this is seen as only possible through the contracting out of these services. It is only through this sub-contracting, it is argued, that 'incentive structures' can be created which can ensure the efficient achievement of desired results. In the sense that public service delivery is, by definition, within this approach, 'delegated to a third party', one wonders in what sense it remains 'public'.

Again, such an approach must lead to a greater role for a new generation of performance service contractors, primarily composed of international non-state actors. The importance of a welfare mix as offering potentials for innovation, for efficiency, and for poverty alleviation, cannot be questioned. However, the focus on sub-contracting as, per se, the only way to achieve efficiency and effectivenss, appears more ideological than evidence-based. Hence, whilst at one level, the new emphasis on coherence and effectiveness within strategic frameworks to alleviate poverty, is a major step forward, there are real problems in the application of new public management approaches and the increased role for non-state actors which it implies.

5. Cases

The original intention was that this Policy Brief would be based, in large part, on continued exploration of issues regarding international non-state actors in a European context. In part, at least, this was to be based on the author's own, ongoing, work in South Eastern Europe. As the research progressed, however, it became clear that the logic of this was problematic given the need to confront global agendas and issues. Instead, two cases are presented here, in summary form, not because of their inherent analytical contribution to the arguments presented here but, rather because they shed light, in a European context, on some of the actors discussed in this paper which may have a relevance for wider contexts. The first case is the work by Caroline de la Porte and Bob Deacon, funded by the Government of Finland, on the role of consulting companies as agents for transfer of EU social policy advice to Eastern Europe, and the second a study, funded by the Open Society Institute, of International Support Policies to Bosnia-Herzegovina.

Box 5.1 Contracting Companies and Consultants[14]

The study: explores the use of sub-contracting by the European Union in its social policy advice to accession candidate countries, looking at the PHARE programme and, in particular CONSENSUS. The research also includes a case study on wider issues of international advice in the making of social policy in Lithuania.

Its Findings Include:
- CONSENSUS more effective than PHARE in terms of advancing the external dimension of EU social policy, although the quality of this varied enormously, most often linked to the quality of individual experts used. ('close to a lottery'[15])
- Diverse group of Contractors interested in participating in the programme; with very diverse motiviations; diverse value-base in social policy; with individual Contractors rarely involving a multi-national group of extenal consultants.
- Broad agreement by interviewees on the 'ideal characteristics' of foreign and local experts.
- Selection processes long, tedious, bureaucratic and not transparent. Feeling that it could be biased in favour of management consultancy companies who can produce "glossy reports and charts"[16].
- Most successful interventions had a broad external vision of reform, integrated into the national reform agenda, with a major role for local experts.

Its Recommendations Include:
- Strengthening the social policy base of EU advice programmes, and ensure that contractors and experts are trained in EU social policy objectives.
- Need to strengthen institutional memory of the track records of contracting organisations and, even more importantly, of individual experts.
- End sub-contracting of project evaluations to increase the institutional memory within EU.
- Essential that experts have previous experience in the recipient country.
- Avoid competitive race to subcontract best local experts and pay local experts more.
- Lengthen consultancy contracts to ensure sustainable and consistent shifts in social policy.
- Increase role for recipient country Ministry and local experts.

Its Significance:
- First major study of role of ICCs in a particular sub-contracting environment.
- Focus on motivations of sub-contractors and experts shows wide diversity.
- Finding that sucessful interventions occur when donor and recipient visions are synchronised and where local actors play a significant role has wider significance for social development

---

[14] de la Porte, Caroline and Deacon, Bob (2002)
[15] de la Porte, Caroline (1999) 'The Manner in Which the EU Shapes Social Policy in the CEEC', Paper presented to GASPP Seminar, Helsinki, December. p. 25.
[16] de la Porte, Caroline and Deacon, Bob (2002) op. cit. p 60.

Box 5.2 International Support Policies: lessons (not) learnt from Bosnia-Herzegovina[17]

The Study: multi-disciplinary analysis of international support to BiH since the Dayton Peace Agreement in 1995, primarily by "the benficiaries of this support and assistance". Explores different sectors: Political; Economic and Financial; Social; Employment and Reconstruction; Higher Education and Science; Legal System; Civil Society; Media; and Human Rights. Also explores trends in international aid policies and makes recommendations for change in a regional context.

Its Findings Include:
- Estimates external assistance post-Dayton to BiH to be in the region of 46-53 billion USD, but with little impact of this expenditure on economic and social sustainability, much less on viable institutions, rule of law, and development of democratic processes.
- Flaws of Dayton Peace Agreement as constitutional settlement compounded by impact of 'market fundamentalism' contributing to a weak state and development of localised ciriminalised social and economic relations, essentially dominated by "patronage and influence-peddling networks and extra-legal profit-making ventures run by the leaderships of the dominant nationalist parties".
- 30% of increase in GDP a result of international assistance. Hence, aid driven growth within a weakened state, with no effective internal stewardship of the economy, and no broad economic strategy, other than failed and corrupt privatisation.
- International assistance has failed to give sufficient attention to social policy within reconstruction and peace-building processes.
- Private aid actors have fuelled an implicit social policy based on relief rather than an overarching framework of effective and equitable social services. Project based support to specific client groups has run parallel with an unsupported public sector used as a conduit for distribution of humantiarian aid.
- World Bank has worked at arm's length and with delayed timtables of social sector support.
- Some recent bilateral programmes beginning to seek to adress over-arching social policy at micro- and macro-levels.
- Democracy assistance has had very mixed results with civil society participation more a product of need for economic survival than pursuit of social justice.
- Whole range of private contractors involved in advice and implementation with little co-ordination or exchange of information.

Its Recommendations Include:
- Need for development aid to strengthen local capacities, to be more transparent, integrated, and co-ordinated.
- Importance of regional economic, political and social space.

Its Significance:
- Holistic study of post-conflict development assistance by experts from recipient country.
- Contributes specific case study to debates about need for transition of key global actors.

---

[17] Papiæ, fiarko (ed.) (2001) *International Support Policies to South-East European Countries: lessons (not) learnt in B-H* Sarajevo: Muller.

6. Recommendations

The approach adopted throughout this text has been to seek to explore 'policy' in a very wide sense, and to situate it in context. It has not been a study of a particular development agency and its practices vis a vis international non-state actors. Recommendations, therefore, also need to be pitched at a very broad level. In this final section, a series of ideas, issues, and recommendations for Finland and like-minded countries are put forward. These are based on the broad approach within the analysis and, therefore, may at times appear to be too vague to be practical and, at other times, where more practical, may already have been thought of, implemented, or improved upon. They are framed in such a way as to stimulate debate rather than to be a fixed agenda. In any case, the entire text has exhibited a skepticism to technical changes as a panacea, suggesting that, more than anything else, a period of intense debate needs to take place with all partners and stakeholders if the progressive elements of the new aid and development regime are to take root.

6.1 Sub-contracting Regimes

Whilst researchers tend to suggest that 'more research is needed', this is definitely the case with the issue of 'sub-contracting' and its role within aid and development. Only through case studies of different agency practices can recommendations for good practice emerge. In a sense, sub-contracting regimes need to be judged from a position which, rather than focusing on cost effectiveness, focuses on ways in which to guarantee the incorporation of lessons learning and the preservation of institutional memories. The processes of aid and, in particular, how far they are untied from an obligation to purchase Western personel or equipment, as well as how far they build genuine local capacity, perhaps the two most important crieria here, need to be studied in much greater depth. A larger research study of the intended and unintended effects of sub-contracting regimes may also reveal a greater debate and concern about this issue amongst development actors than may appear to be the case at first sight. It is, certainly, a major topic of informal discussion. Further, empowering developing country governments and civil society organisations to explore the room for maneouvre within sub-contracting regimes would also seem to be important.

6.2 Quality Control – Registers, Standards and Benchmarking

There is widespread recognition that a more diverse aid and development system needs to be based upon a much greater attention to quality control, at the micro-level of individual consultancies, contracts and projects. For some considerable time, sections of the INGO community, particularly those involved in humanitarian aid, have been engaged in efforts to promote self-regulation and, in particular, to incorporate acceptance of agreed minimum standards within this work[18]. In fact, it is far from an easy matter to translate minimum standards in the humanitarian field into other development contexts, although the movement towards standards in all spheres of human service activity should not, and must not, pass development agencies by. It would not seem to be over-constraining for annual registers of organisations, including INGOs and consultancy companies, to be kept, either within donor agencies or co-ordinating bodies such as the DAC, which contained broad information on their interests and track record.

Perhaps more controversially, but in many ways more importantly, there is a need for a register of individual consultants since, in a sub-contracted aid market, it is the role of such actors which are increasingly important. At the moment, such registers are kept by some development agencies, but mainly for the purpose of ensuring that suitably qualified consultants can be identified for short-term assignments at short notice. It may be possible to expand and formalise these registers to ensure a greater degree of 'appraisal' of consultants' performance, based on best practice of internal staff appraisal (entrance and exit interviews; learning issues; appraisals by contracting agency, by the consultant, and by various stakeholders; and so on). Ultimately, might it not be conceivable that consultants would have to obtain a certificate of competence in international development, renewable annually, in order to be eligible for contracts? At the moment, there are assumptions that some 'expert' consultants have nothing to learn, coupled with a high degree of informal 'word of mouth' scrutiny of consultants.

A linked, but rarely discussed issue, concerns the implications of consultancy modes for gender mainstreaming. In the absence of any research evidence, it could be wrong to pursue this issue in too great a detail. However, the author's own experience of international consultancy assignments suggests that disproportionate numbers of men are engaged as consultants. It may be that this relates only to one particular field, social policy consultancy, in one particular place, South Eastern Europe. However, at the very least, enuring that aggregated figures for consultancy assignments include gender data would bring this aspect of work closer to development agencies' routine gender monitoring and equal opportunities requirements.

There is a need to couple standards with issues of codes of ethics, transparency, and clear mission statements. Again, whilst this has begun to occur in the humanitarian field, there is much less attention to it in development contexts. At the moment,

---

[18] Weiss, Thomas (1999) op. cit. p. 22 refers to the Sphere Humanitarian Charter and Minimum Standards.

practices of 'body shopping' – finding the best cvs to win a proposal; and of 'body swapping' – moving from one type of contract with one agency to another in a different field; tend to be subject to very little control. Above all, the need for cumulative evaluation of the performance of all external development actors, in particular countries, in regions, and according to particular themes, would be of immense importance in building much greater learning into all development organisations.

The issue of transparency also relates to pricing. Of course, competitive tendering suggests that pricing is a matter between the contractor and contractee. However, the need to discuss pricing issues collectively and, perhaps, reach a broad level of agreement might help to avoid a situation where differential pricing leads to unintended effects in terms of capacity issues, amongst international agencies and between those agencies and local actors, counterparts and stakeholders. The issue of the uninentended effects of high salaries for international and local staff or of international agencies, also needs to be addressed, particularly in emergency environments.

6.3 Backing the Local

'Trusting the local' has long been the mantra of the international development community. However, the logic of sub-contracting has not been adjusted accordingly. A fundamental shift in thinking is needed so that the involvement of any actors outside of a local environment and situation needs to be carefully justified at every stage, including project design, project, development, tendering and implementation. The 'value added' of, initially, regionally-based organisations, groups and individuals followed by those outside of the region, should be explicitly stated and justified in all project documentation so as to minimise a kind of implicit 'foreign is best' modality which creeps into a project simply because of the realities of sub-contracting and tendering.

If the trend is to longer term programmes then this requires real capacity building of local partners and an explicit recognition, built into programmes, of a decreasing, strategically oriented, external capacity building component. It also requires direct support for new organsiations to emerge who can play a leadership role in development projects in the medium- term. This should be the goal of framework partnership agreements which could require demonstration of increasing work and responsibility for local actors over a given time period. It also may mean encouraging more flexibility in terms of swapping and twinning arrangements so that local stakeholders are able to play decision-making roles in Northern development agencies.

6.4 From Poverty Reduction to Social Rights

If there is increasing attention to poverty reduction, then this must be in a wider structural framework and, above all, one which gives attention to issues of social rights. Much of the most recent thinking on issues of poverty, already embrace wider questions of social exclusion and inequality. This suggests the need for analysis of livelihoods, social justice and social rights, including the importance of universal entitlements, going far beyond the current emphasis on basic education and primary health care. A social rights perspective needs to continually move between micro-, meso- and macro-levels so that the links between issues of governance, provision, innovation, access and voice are continually addressed.

Perhaps above all, partnerships for social justice cannot be technical but, rather, must involve attention to power issues. In this way, allies can be found amongst international non-state actors, providing many of the 'rules of the game' are changed in the interests of a genuine move to a more inclusive globalisation. As stated in other policy briefs, part of this must involve Ministries or Departments of Aid and Social Development ensuring that Foreign and Trade Ministries also understand these shifts, and are engaged with a range of international, regional and local non state actors. The Government of Finland can play a leading role in articulating a vision which is responsive to the critiques of globalisation as disenfranchising large parts of the world and a leader in a new dialogue for global social justice. Many in the international aid and development community would be responsive to such a lead.

Acknowledgements

I wish to thank Bob Deacon and Meri Koivusalo for constructive comments on earlier drafts of this paper. In addition, the research assistance of Minna Ilva, and her enthusiasm and tireless willingness to answer yet more requests over email, was invaluable in the writing of this paper. Responsibility for contents is mine alone.

Paul Stubbs
Zagreb, November 2002

References

Biekhart, K. (1999), *The Politics of Civil Society Building: European private agencies and democratic transitions in Central America*, International books, Utrecht.

Black, M. (1996), *Children First: The Story of UNICEF, Past and Present*, Oxford University Press.

Boli, J. and Thomas, G. (eds) (1999), *Constructing World Culture International Non-Governmental Organizations Since 1875,* Stanford University Press, Stanford CA.

Brook, P. and Smith, S. (Eds.) (2002), *Contracting for Public Services: output-based aid and its applications,* World Bank, Washington.

Burnell, P. (2000), Democracy Assistance: origins and organizations, In *Democracy Assistance: international co-operation for democratization* (Ed, Burnell, P.) Frank Cass, London.

Carothers, T. (1999), *Aiding Democracy Abroad: the learning curve,* Carnegie Endowment for International Peace, Washington DC.

Castells, M. (1996), *The Rise of the Network Society,* Blackwell, Oxford.

Chabbott, C. (1999), Development INGOs, in: Boli, J. and Thomas, G. (eds) (1999), *Constructing World Culture: International Non-Governmental Organizations Since 1875,* Stanford University Press, Stanford CA., pp. 222-248

Cooke, B. and Kothari, U. (eds) (2001), *Participation: the new tyranny,* Zed Books, London.

Cornwall, A. and Gaventa, J. (2000), "From Users and Choosers to Makers and Shapers: repositioning participation in social policy", *IDS Bulletin,* vol. 21, no. 4, p. 56.

Cowater website (2002), http://www.cowater.com, (Accessed October 2002).

de la Porte, C. (1999), "The Manner in Which the EU Shapes Social Policy in the CEEC", Paper presented to GASPP Seminar, December 1999, Helsinki.

de la Porte, C. and Deacon, B. (2002), *Contracting Companies and Consultants; the EU and social policy of Accession Countries,* GASPP Occasional Paper 9, Stakes, Helsinki.

Deacon, B. (Ed.) (2000), *Civil Society, NGOs and Global Governance,* GASPP Occasional Paper 7, Stakes, Helsinki.

Deacon, B. (2000), Globalisation: a threat to equitable social provision?, *IDS Bulletin,* vol. 21, no. 4, p. 37.

Deacon, B. (2002), *Global Social Governance Reform,* GASPP Policy Brief 1, Stakes, Helsinki.

Deacon, B., Hulse, M. and Stubbs, P. (1997), *Global Social Policy: international organizations and the future of welfare,* Sage, London.

Developmentex.com (2002), www.developmentex.com.

Donini, A. (1996), The Bureaucracy and the Free Spirits: stagnation and innovation in the relationship between the UN and NGOs, in: Weiss, T. and Gordenker, L (eds), *NGOs, the UN and Global Governance,* Lynne Reiner, Boulder.

Duffield, M. (1996), *Social Reconstruction in Croatia and Bosnia: an exploratory report for SIDA,* University of Birmingham.

GOPA (2002), http://www.gopa.de, (Accessed October 2002).

Gordenker, L. and Weiss, T. (1999), Pluralizing Global Governance, in: Gordenker, L. and Weiss, T. (eds), *NGOs, the UN and Global Governance,* Lynne Reiner, Boulder.

Gough, I. (2001), "Globalization and welfare regimes: the East Asian case", *Global Social Policy,* vol. 1 no. 2, pp. 163-190.

Gough, I. (2002), *Adapting Welfare Regimes to Development Contexts,* Unpublished.

Guidry, J., Kennedy, M. and Zald, M. (eds) (2000), *Globalization and Social Movements: culture, power and the transnational public sphere,* University Press, Michigan.

Hulme, D. and Edwards, M. (eds) (1997), *NGOs, States and Donors: too close for comfort?,* Mcmillan, Basingstoke.

Keck, M. and Sikkink, K. (1998), *Activists Beyond Borders: advocacy networks in international policy,* Cornell University Press, Ithaca.

Koivusalo, M. (1999), *World Trade Organization and Trade-Creep in Health and Social Policies,* GASPP

Occasional Paper 4, Stakes, Helsinki.

Korten, D. (1990), *Getting to the 21st Century: voluntary action and the global agenda,* Kumarian Press, West Harford.

Lucas, H. and Cornwall, A. (2002), "Researching Social Policy", Paper presented to IDS Social Policy Conference, March 2002, Brighton.

Madon, S. (2000), *International NGOs: networking, information flows and learning,* , IDPM: Manchester.

Marshal, A. and al, e. (2001), *Policies to Roll Back the State and Privatise?: poverty reduction strategy papers investigated,* World Development Movement, London.

Meyer, J. et al (1997), "World Society and the Nation State", *American Journal of Sociology,* vol. 103, no. 1, pp. 144-181.

Mkandawire, T. (1998), *Notes on Consultancy andRresearch in Africa,* Centre for Development Research, Copenhagen.

Nelson, P. (2000), Internationalising Economic and Environmental Policy: transnational NGO networks and the World Bank's expanding influence, in: Vandersluis, S. and Yeros, P. (eds) *Poverty in World Politics: whose global era?,* Macmillan, Basingstoke.

OECD (1996), *Directory of Non-Governmental Organisations Active in Sustainable Development,* OECD Development Centre, Paris.

OECD (2001), *DAC Guidelines on Poverty Reduction,* OECD/DAC, Paris.

Overseas Development Administration (1995), *Social Policy Research for Development,* ODA/ESCOR.

Papic, Z. (ed) (2001), *International Support Policies to South-East European Countries: lessons (not) learnt in B-H,* Muller, Sarajevo.

Ramia, G. (2002), "Global Social Policy, INGOs and the Importance of Strategic Management", *Global Social Policy,* forthcoming.

Ritchie, R. et al (1999), "A Brand New World for Nonprofits", *International Journal of Nonprofit and Voluntary Sector Marketing,* vol. 4, no.1.

Robinson, M. (1997), Privatising the voluntary sector: NGOs as public service contractors?, in: Hulme, D. and Edwards, M. (eds), *NGOs, States and Donors: too close for comfort?,* Macmillan, Basingstoke.

Staffs of the World Bank and the International Monetary Fund (2002), *Review of the PRSP Approach; interim findings,* IDA/IMF, 15 March .

Stubbs, P. (2000), Partnership or colonisation? the relationships between international agencies and local NGOs in Bosnia-Herzegovina, in: Deacon, B. (ed) *Civil Society, NGOs and Global Governance,* GASPP Occasional Paper 7, Stakes, Helsinki.

Stubbs, P. (2002), "Globalisation , memory and welfare regimes in transition: towards an anthropology of transnational policy transfers", *International Journal of Social Welfare,* forthcoming.

UNRISD (2000), *Visible Hands: taking responsibility for Social Development,* UNRISD, Geneva.

Wedel, J. (2001), *Collision and collusion: the strange case of Western aid to Eastern Europe,* Palgrave, New York.

Weiss, T. (1999), *International NGOs, Global Governance, and Social Policy in the UN System,* GASPP Occasional Paper 3, Stakes, Helsinki.

Wood, G. (2000), "Prisoners and Escapees: improving the institutional responsibility square in Bangladesh", *Public Administration and Development,* vol. 20, pp. 221-37.

Woods, A. (2000), *Facts about European NGOs Active in International Development,* OECD Development Centre, Paris, p.33.

Woods, A. (2000), What Role for the Multilateral Institutions, Donors and NGOs in the New Framework for Poverty Eradication, in: Deacon, B. (ed), *Civil Society, NGOs and Global Governance,* GASPP Occasionl Paper 7, Stakes, Helsinki.